D1128903

UNCORRECTED ADVANCE PROOF

Title:	**BEFORE OUR EYES:** *New and Selected Poems, 1975-2017*
Author:	Eleanor Wilner
US Publication Date:	September 2019
ISBN:	978-0-691-19332-8 Cloth $45.00 - £37.95 978-0-691-19333-5 Paper $17.95 - £14.95
Pages:	232 pages, 6 1/8 x 9 1/4

Agency/Agent info: N/A

For additional information or questions, please contact:
Julia Haav, Assistant Publicity Director
Tel 609-258-2831
Fax 609-258-1335
julia_haav@press.princeton.edu

PRINCETON UNIVERSITY PRESS
41 William Street, Princeton, NJ 08540
(609) 258-3897 Phone, (609) 258-1335 FAX

In Europe contact:
Caroline Priday, Global Director of Publicity
Caroline_Priday@press.princeton.edu
Princeton University Press
6 Oxford Street
Woodstock, England
OX20 1TR
Tel +44 (0) 1993 814503
Fax+44 (0) 1993 814504

BEFORE OUR EYES
New and Selected Poems, 1975-2017

Eleanor Wilner

BEFORE OUR EYES gathers more than thirty new poems by Eleanor Wilner, along with representative selections from her seven previous books, to present a major overview of her distinguished body of work. A poet who engages with history in lyrical language, Wilner creates worlds that reflect on and illuminate the actual one, drawing on the power of communal myth and memory to transform them into agents of change.

In these poems, well-known figures step out of old texts to alter their stories and new figures arise out of the local air—a girl with a fury of bees in her hair, homesick statues who step down from their pedestals, a bat cave whose altar bears a judgment on our worship of war, and a frog whose spring wakening invites our own. In the process, ancient myths are naturalized while nature is newly mythologized in the service of life.

BEFORE OUR EYES features widely anthologized works such as "Sarah's Choice" and "Reading the Bible Backwards." In the new poems, Wilner records the bewildering public shocks of the current moment, when civic life is under threat, when language itself is attacked, and when poetry's lens of collective imagination becomes a way to resist falsity, to seek meaning, and to really see what is before our eyes.

Eleanor Wilner is the author of seven previous collections of poetry, most recently *Tourist in Hell* and *The Girl with Bees in Her Hair*. In 2019, she received the Frost Medal for distinguished lifetime achievement in poetry, the highest award presented by the Poetry Society of America. Her other awards include the Juniper Prize, three Pushcart Prizes, and a fellowship from the MacArthur Foundation, and her work appears in many anthologies, including *The Best American Poetry*. She teaches in the MFA Program for Writers at Warren Wilson College, and lives in Philadelphia.

SEPTEMBER
978-0-691-19332-8 Cloth $45.00 - £37.95
978-0-691-19333-5 Paper $17.95 - £14.95
232 pages. 6 1/8 x 9 1/4.
POETRY | LITERARY COLLECTIONS

BEFORE OUR EYES

PRINCETON SERIES OF CONTEMPORARY POETS

Susan Stewart, series editor

For other titles in the Princeton Series of Contemporary Poets see page [? XX]

BEFORE OUR EYES

New and Selected Poems: 1975–2017

Eleanor Wilner

PRINCETON UNIVERSITY PRESS
Princeton & Oxford

Copyright © 2019 by Eleanor Wilner

Requests for permission to reproduce material from this work
should be sent to permissions@press.princeton.edu

Published by Princeton University Press

41 William Street, Princeton, New Jersey 08540

6 Oxford Street, Woodstock, Oxfordshire OX20 1TR

press.princeton.edu

All Rights Reserved

LCCN

ISBN: 978-0-691-19332-8

ISBN (pbk.): 978-0-691-19333-5

British Library Cataloging-in-Publication Data is available

Editorial: Anne Savarese and Thalia Leaf

Production Editorial: Ellen Foos

Text Design: Pamela Schnitter

Jacket/Cover Design: {~?~or Text and Jacket/Cover Design—PE to adjust as needed}
{~?~PE: Credit the designer regardless of whether they are in-house or freelance.
Freelance jacket designer credits can be found in the Jacket Art Credit Line field of
the Copy & Jacket Circ dashboard.}

Production: Merli Guerra

Publicity:{~?~to come}

Copyeditor: Jodi Beder

Jacket/Cover Credit:

This book has been composed in Adobe Garamond Pro and Scala Sans

Printed on acid-free paper. ∞

Printed in the United States of America

10 9 8 7 6 5 4 3 2 1

TO THE CONTINUING PRESENCE OF

CLAUDIA EMERSON (1957–2014)

MICHELLE BOISSEAU (1955–2017)

TONY HOAGLAND (1953–2018)

CONTENTS

ACKNOWLEDGMENTS

WITH thanks to the editors of the following publications in which these poems first appeared.

Asheville Poetry Review: "An Answering Music to Lines by Sam Hamill"

Birmingham Poetry Review: "Intimations," Moonlit Wake," "The Phoenix Reflects on Its Peculiar Situation," "What the Kite Sees," and "When Vision Narrows to a Single Beam of Light"

Fiddlehead (Canada): "Gnawed Bone, Covered Bridge," "In Memoriam," and "The Aquarium"

New England Review: "Shells"

New Ohio Review: "To Think of How Cold," and "Underworld"

Poetry: "Ars Poetica, 2017"

Prairie Schooner: "Turning"

Scoundrel Time (online): "Elegy in Glass and Stone"

Spillway: "For the First Time," "Bird's Eye View, Close-up," and "Tracking"

The Drunken Boat (online): "Blue Reflection"

The Hampden-Sydney Poetry Review: "Sowing," and "Writing in Sand While Walking in Walt's Footprints"

"Sowing" was reprinted in *The Best American Poetry 2014*, guest ed. Terrance Hayes; series ed. David Lehman (New York: Scribner, 2014).

"To Think of How Cold" was reprinted in *The Best American Poetry 2016*, guest ed. Edward Hirsch, series ed. David Lehman (New York: Scribner, 2016).

"Endings, from a Verse by Gwendolyn Brooks" first appeared in *The Golden Shovel Anthology*, ed. Peter Kahn, Ravi Shankar, and Patricia Smith (University of Arkansas Press, 2017).

"Parable of the Eyes" and "The Photographer on Assignment" first appeared in *Truth to Power: Writers Respond to the Rhetoric of Hate and Fear* (*Cutthroat, A Journal of the Arts*, 2017)

"Before Our Eyes" and "The Uses of What Is Hollow" first appeared in *The Eloquent Poem*, ed. Elise Paschen (New York: Persea, 2019).

To the Great Dead who were my teachers; to Dr. Richard A. Macksey—my one living, irreplaceable teacher. And with unending gratitude and love to the friends poetry has brought me, especially those, gone too soon, to whom this book is dedicated; the writers of the MFA Program for Writers at Warren Wilson College and the GG circle of poets from Centrum; to the poets of the Cliff Notes Writing Conference, Boulder, Utah; to Marcia Pelletiere, my order-bringer; to Carolyn Creedon Andrews for her keen eye and invaluable help in editing and preparing this manuscript; to poet David Lee for being my found brother; to Susan Stewart, who has for so many years been a champion of these poems; to Joan Liftin, compañera; to Trudy, Mike, Noah, and Molly, the family I was given who are exactly the family I would have chosen; to Bob, my haven.

In a dark time, the eye begins to see ...

—THEODORE ROETHKE

NEW POEMS (2011–2017)

1 *Fair is foul, and foul is fair*

WHEN VISION NARROWS TO
A SINGLE BEAM OF LIGHT

For years he had been hidden, quiet,
huge head on his paws,
almost a sphinx in his composure,
a figure waiting
for a breeze to move the dense
green canopy of leaves overhead,
enough to bring a hair-thin laser line
of light down
        into the endless twilight
below;
        he had been patient, waiting
for the underbrush to open, for a low
wind to enter, ruffling his fur, astir
along his spine, then a gravelly
purr within, slowly
the pink
mouth
opening
into a yawn . . .
if you were not afraid
you could see how the light
makes his wet teeth shine
as he runs his tongue along them,
how his languid stretching shoves aside
years of debris the forest shed,
dry leaves like dead laws,
how his claws unfurl as he breaches
the hedge that had held him close, how

this small wind,
                  this one thin line of light suffices
to open the waking tiger to our view—
that line of light a burning fuse
meant to measure
the diminishing distance
between the tiger
and us.

TRACKING

(*pace* Robert Frost)

No light in the woods, a cold rain
falls, damp penetrating every cell,
lichens spread, mushrooms push up
their blind, gray heads; at every step
your feet sink into the soaking loam,
the chill deepens, no way to keep warm,
nowhere to rest, and too much rain
to make a fire, and high above, a circling
shape—a thrumming sound: the drones
are tracking, even here. You thought that
where the trails diverged, if you found
the way that those who went before
had gone, you might escape—*Though*
  as for that the passing there had worn
  them really about the same.

So any choice had been absurd,
based on little but the need to move,
old maps, a hunch, the flip of a coin,
while the sound overhead beat
its alarm (was it real, or in your head?),
it followed the way that you had gone,
and *something* was tearing the leaves up there—
whirring, setting the nerves on edge,
the rain falling, a slant wind driving it
into your face, and the markers
missing, though the others had gone
this way before, of that you felt sure,
and none had come back, not one

had come back.

         You stumble forward
along the path, like one who is carrying
a message in code to a city under siege,
a city that may have succumbed
to disease, or hunger, or fire, or worse . . .
yet still the message burns in your hand,
in spite of all, it impels your flight,
though the rains fall, the path darkens,
the drone is loud and panic threatens—
you go on, you brush the dripping
branches away, you shout a curse
at the tracking drone, you have
lost the path, you go on.

THE AQUARIUM

As we are standing by a tank
    its glass has caught the faces
of us all   ephemeral on the solid glass
    a spectral crowd   our eyes look back at us
away from what we're gazing at   the lustrous
    cruising bodies of the captive fish
that circle endlessly   in the enormous glowing
    tube in which caught species swim . . .
we watch the glittering victims
    of our showcase appetite   and for
the flashing fins of passing things
    we watch   our fading faces   watching us . . .

        where to place the eyes
in such a scene   its endless back and forth
    so circumscribed   trapped on the tank's
reflective glass   imprisoned in its lit
    transparent case   detainees
of the deep   shimmering faces   where
    through each other's masks   we see
the bodies turn   and turn again   to fit
    the walls of glass   our faces shift and flicker
in the pulsing waves of light   the water throws
    this glimmering show   with nowhere
else to go   the gaze is locked in place
    fixed on itself   and all the life inside
comes round again   again   and circles back

UNDERWORLD

The black mouth opens in the white
façade, our boat slides in; at first
it's dark in the tunnel, a motor hums,
the little boat cuts the black water
like a fin,
        we're caught in a Möbius strip
of song, closed curve, it must go on, and on,
and suddenly, round the bend they come
from some drenched honeycomb
in which the poisoned bees are caught
and spun,
        and now, they're all around us,
in the glowing artificial light, turning slowly
on their stands, staring with the fixed and
painted grin of dolls, a music box world
that turns and turns, wound-up dolls
and windmill blades, in a stupor
of cheer and hidden gears,
which hold them in a common grip,
and as they spin, they seem to sing,
because they're *made* to seem to sing,
the song is all the world they're in—
                the walls
breathe damp as our boat slides by
kitsch pagodas, cuckoo clocks,
a Taj Mahal, grass skirts hula hula
under ersatz palms—
        the curving tunnel moves us on,
we sense dark waters churn below
as we pass the whirl of dressed-up dolls,

dressed as if for a costume ball, who spin
and sing, and sing and spin,

                             around they go,
beguiling, infantile, and dead: each
with the same round head, wide eyes,
so clean and sweet—

                    as if below
the killing fields of history's endless
wars, Elysium's bright waterways
forever wind, filled with blissful
little dolls, androids all, in the singing
tunnels of the underworld—

                        a sign
reminds us to keep our heads down,
and our hands inside the boat,
as the walls close in, the dolls sing on,
dum   dedum dum   dum dedum,
dum   dedum dum   dum dedum . . .

THE PHOTOGRAPHER ON ASSIGNMENT

Election, 2016

Owl scream, restless sleep, Alaska's
midnight sun, high noon all night, unnatural
to the body's mind. The camera falters
in my hand. And I am cold, observing here
so near the pole, where, all summer, the sun
is sleepless, but the night is cold, even the shutter
sticks from the cold, stutters, deep disquiet
in the veins, as I watch the she-owl
guarding her young, beaks an open-mouthed Y
of hunger. No cover in this tundra but low shrub,
too long a winter has kept life close
to the ground, where the lemmings thrive,
plentiful in the stunted grass. I watch
the owl soar on opened wings, hunting
while the female guards the nest; again
and again he strikes—lemming after lemming,
and since the sun stays up, the lemmings
stand revealed; they don't conceal themselves
but hope to warn their predators away
with their small, fanged aggression—
                                    easy targets, all.
In the unforgiving light, the owl
spins overhead, talons open as he dives—
the lemmings pile up; the nestlings, stuffed,
can eat no more, but, his prey so eager, so exposed,
the owl keeps hunting, lemming after lemming
dropping from his claws.

The sun burns, the owl hunts,
the lemmings are a bleeding pile
of useless flesh and fur
that grows and grows
beside the sated nest.
That is the photo I bring home: a monument
to the harvest of that white night.

PARABLE OF THE EYES

Post-election, 2016

Somewhere in America, on the plains,
is a silo full of eyes.
                          They are closed,
shut tight, though, now and then, a few
tears run, and a rivulet of salty water
shudders the piles in the murk
of that great bin, like storage lockers
where people put things, stuff they can't
remember why they bought—once
valued things that got in the way
as they moved from here to there,
and there to here:
                          here, where the bells toll
day and night—deep bronze the sound,
its slow decay goes on and on,
and the eyeless try to drown the sound,
sit down to the TV news, when
the knock of the fist comes on the door,
and you can hear the grinding of gears
as the trucks pull up outside,
                          and the eyes, locked in
the heartland silo, suddenly blink
and open wide, and all they see
are other eyes
in all that darkness
staring back.

ELEGY IN GLASS AND STONE

Crows working the ground,
picking at husks. Harvest
one place starves the rest,
crosswinds can't be read,
and nothing can parse
the syntax of the soul.
Listen: it's the thin wail
of a world gone wrong;
what takes cover under
the tongue is the song
that won't be sung, the
waters are rising, the sun
has sunk behind the many-
storied towers of glass,
catching the last ver-
million light; inside,
rooms an empty cash
write-off, sheets of glass
a sheath around vacancy.
Nothing breathes inside.
Below, the wind picks up
a plastic bag and fills it
like a sail; it spins across
our line of sight, is caught
and replicated in those
thousand panes of glass,
the walls become a tower
of animated trash. So close
to Wall St. now, you can
almost hear the crash.

Out
    there,
        as
       Liberty
       lifts
     her torch of
     gold, cold
    on her island
   rock, Ishmael,
  carrying the drowned
Queequeg in his arms, stumbles
with his burden to the shore.

DAEDALUS, THE EXILE, THINKS OF HIS SON

It wasn't the sun. Or that he flew too high—
lots of boys do that, and live;
   it wasn't that he didn't hear me, his father,
shout to warn him;
   it wasn't that he was boy and dream and muscle
and sheathed sword;
   it was whose son he was, not one of theirs.
So, as he circled above them,
      wings spread, in the pure delight of feeling
      free—it enraged them;
they ranted, they recoiled, they took aim.

         In the labyrinth
I built for the creature, the prison that became
my own, the central chamber is empty now,
its straw moldy, the creature has fled;
I, who alone knew the plan
of those bewildering corridors, returned.
I led him out. His is the huge, horned
shadow you see, moving always a little ahead
of you, always a little ahead
         of whatever happens next.

UNDER THE TABLE

*The production of sound signals by body rapping or drumming . . .
occurs most commonly in colonies that occupy wooden or carton
nests . . . workers of the carpenter ants . . . can be launched into
drumming by any sign that their nest has been breached.*

—FROM *THE ANTS* BY HÖLLDOBLER AND WILSON

Did it stand always so, three good legs, one wobbling
      if you tried to lean, adding the least hint of weight
to this survivor marked with scars—burn holes
      of cigarettes, wood pocked by bullets, time-trace,
beginning rot, snow, spring thaw, ice again: how many
      times did the earth turn while the stained table stood,
half-submerged in vines, lichen, the droppings of birds, fungus,
      nearly lost in undergrowth, among the spindly trees
thinned too many times by the axe, but thick again in number;
      abandoned in these woods, the table stood
so far from any house or habitation . . .
                              as if some family game
      or meal had suddenly been interrupted—a furious
crash, a door kicked in, shouts, helmeted men,
the cries, the useless pleas, (the held breath)
please, and then, their butchery complete, they took
      their leave of what was left . . .
                              from under the table
where he had hidden, the boy must have crawled, and later,
      dragged it out the door, out into the woods, away
from the horror the house had become—the table his
      refuge for days; at last, the house he set
afire burned, and with it, sanctuary, hope:
      a blaze that was his only way to make it disappear, release

what held him there. He set off then, along a track to anywhere,
    and those who walked with him, walked in silence,
for the dead cannot speak without drinking
    the blood of the newly slain, and they were
thirsty, they were so very thirsty . . .

Where the table had been, the underbrush blooms,
the forest has taken it back—rain, rot, vermin,
vines—all of it gone to earth again, down where
moles tunnel through the underground, dens
crammed with worms their saliva has stunned,
for winter is coming, and the ants drum.

BLUE REFLECTION

Wading   in the shallows   of America
     on a fall day   the sun bright   and trying
       in the big empty
           up there   for cheer
       the heron freezes
         studying
       his reflection
      watching for the flicker
    (below his growing doubt)   that means fish
the creek has a chemical smell   is thin   filled in when
       rains brought the mud down   from the banks
the water has an oily sheen   and this year   silence hangs over the scene
   deserted   by insects and frogs   To this stream   the heron had
     always returned   but now   his hunger bids him   fly
in a swift rush of wings   he's airborne   growing smaller
until all that is left   is a blue figure   in the faded grass
       at memory's edge   mirage
   as if time's arrow bent   turned back   the shrunken creek
recovers its rush   the stream clears   insects hum   the fish swim
   into abundance again   as the blue image of the heron
       riding the slipstream   of reality's departure
glides down from the past   and   wings folded like origami
     lands back in the reeds   more ours now   than nature's
   hybrid made   of letters   flesh and wish   poised to strike
     focused   on its reflection   shuddering in
       a sudden wind on the water's
back   a tearing noise
     the image is dashed
         broken   as his neck
     unfurls   he strikes
         raises his head
          beak clamped
            on an agony of silver—
       what   like mercury
    can't be held   or helped
and   swallowed   is poison

THE PHOENIX REFLECTS ON
ITS PECULIAR SITUATION

Beauty is a word that other birds should fear,
                  already desired for their flesh,
        then, for the beauty of their feathers' iridescence.
How slim their necks, how soon they break. I pity
their condition, and desire it: for I am the fire's child,
heir to a thousand ills because I cannot die. I have lately
been hearing only the static of dragon-speech,
        harsh clamor fills the air, the ear—
                the clapping of metal hands, loose shingles
        on a cosmic roof, the idiot speech that fills my brain
as the centuries pass, as I rise again
              from the ardent embrace of the flames.
    How I've come to fear the horror
that recurs, that lasts a thousand years and then,
in fire, returns, repeats—fire
at the planet's core, its beauty at the heart of war—
how I could wish an end to repetition,
to what each time sounds new—a trumpet's call
to Glory—the blood is stirred,
the slow pulse of peace forever lost—my glorious
body rising from the flames, its armored sheen
so blinding . . .
          and I am fearful tired;
my feathers, once a shimmer of gold, grow dull,
their ends are frayed, the bones in my long
and once-proud neck grow frail, they splinter at a touch,
the plume that rose above my head hangs limp,
and what I fear, and fear it most, is fire—
its siren call to savagery, the way men run to it,

their faces leering like those at Bosch's suffering Christ, lit
in the glow, and I, blood-red and gleaming gold, rising
to adorn the tyrant's rule, fury reborn in flames . . .

Enough. This time they'll find me in the embers
of what was once a place—at peace,
            a pile of wet and ruined feathers in the rain.
                        Amen.

TURNING

Some days it was nothing more than a whine
in the wires when the wind plays
the power lines like a long complaint;
sometimes it was the sound of shuffling cards,
the click of thrown dice, the slight percussion
of bum luck; or the ice-struck days when silence
was a jar with the lid screwed tight, and all
you could see was a huge eye staring in at you,
cyclopean, cold blue, an incurious malice,
slightly veiled by the blur of breath on glass.

Out here, the air is clearing now,
    a slow return of what has been
shaken from slumbering in the dark,
    as a bear, sleepy and bemused, stumbles
into the sun in early spring, the frost
    still on the morning grass, but the winter
freeze that held the earth in its bitter fist
    opened now, and the bear, hungry and not yet
quite awake, rubs her winter eyes
    with a warming paw, feels a world begin
to sharpen itself against her claws,
    and hears a few long notes
that might have been a bird, if birds
    could hold a note like that,
the brass horn of the sun raised
    against the night, the slow return of blood
to the waking flesh, a prickling all along the legs,
    the spine, and high above the pine's long

branch, green through all the time of white,
a song, not of a bird, but just what, invisible
calls forth mass
from the passing particles
and spins a world from elegance
and chance, embodied like the Hindu
gods who, having just destroyed the world
that they had made, don't stop
to rue what they must always do, but dance,
and spin the cosmos like a monstrous top,
and so it all begins again,
and as it spins,
the dice
like
distant thunder,
roll.

II   An Answering Music

IN MEMORIAM

On pain of death,
scratch pictures in the dust.

—ELEANOR ROSS TAYLOR

Having left
            open
the windows   the door
      she left the place
to air   whatever the weather
      chose to make of it

On her way   stopped   one last time
      by an old logging road
ruts long since
worn smooth   it ran
to a third-growth   spindly woods
(no one alive
who could recall
                  even
      the ghostly grandeur of the first)

Drew the stick
once more across
the blank face
                  of the dust
Entranced
      by her task   athirst   scratched
the protean script
   figures   a blur

obscured   by the slightest breath
              as if   the obdurate stick
      to write   required the dust
and dust   to speak of itself   the wind

WINGSPAN

Hope said Emily (her life now
versions in anyone's mouth—
the plaything of posterity,
as we are shaken in the moment's
lawless jaws, white and lethal as
the crocodile's teeth) *is a thing
with feathers*, but so few, so blue,
and such short wings, vestigial,
it was not meant to fly
but to abide, here, deep in leaves,
thick in the scent of summer green,
the air dusted with pollen;
nearby, the long drumroll of the surf,
and there, under the sky's immensity of blue,
a scatter of feathers on the ocean waves
where wide-winged Icarus flew.

HOMAGE

*They cawed full voiced / and would have released him from his /
bindings had their beaks held their power /and had there been
time in that place.*

—VIEVEE FRANCIS

Words under your spell. Like your namesake St. Francis,
in cahoots with the birds, you have seen the scarecrow,
the image of Suffering, of the cruelty men visit on
what makes them feel, what cowers within them;
known the compassion of crows, unashamed of their
voices; known the dove, with its soft cooing, has nothing
to offer, choking as it is on the remnant of green
from the flood that is coming.
                              The ragged figure of straw,
stretched on crossed sticks, is throbbing with wings,
a mercy of crows who've abandoned the fields, fit only
for gleaning (while grain rots in the towering silos);
their cawing a calling as sweet and unlikely as what's
drawn from the hive in the tree's hidden hollow,
that wounded place from which something was taken,
and the queen and her swarm found it—even from here,
you can hear the hum, for there is time in this place, time
taking the sun with it, leaving honey, a murmur of bees,
evensong's praise, long shadows searching the ground.

ANOTHER ALLEGORY OF THE CAVE

It was night in Plato's cave, the shackled prisoners,
there to prove a point—that he has seen the light,
is their redeemer, and so should be their king.
They spoke among themselves, and it was hard
to make out words at first, so softly did they speak,
conspirators after all, against the one whose plot
had locked their shackles, yoked their gaze,
and lit the fires behind them, set
the shadows dancing on the walls. (And must
have smiled at his conceit, his perfect illustration.)

And so, caught in his design, they only saw
what they were forced to see, while he,
when he would come to set them free, dressed
as he would be in ruler's robes, assumed
their gratitude to him for their return to Truth—
high above, the ideal form, white orb of fire,
to which he'd bid them look, as he had done.
His eyes were cinders now, blinded
by annihilating light, the cornea blistered
and cracked, the retina detached, sight
gone while standing in a surfeit of pure sun.

The cave is open now; its portals hung
        with beads; you can move freely in and out
the way the fingers play against the strings
        idly, of a quiet afternoon, no melodies,
just runs of notes, and sometimes chords
        or a discordant phrase never to resolve,

veils restless in air, the lightest breeze,
        the sun at a slant, throwing our shadows,
longer now, against the deep-dyed carpets,
        their intricate, unreadable designs:
Hamadan, Mashad, Keshan, Shiraz, Tabriz.

SOWING

*. . . she glided from the sky and ordered him / to plow the ground
and then to plant within / the earth, the serpent's teeth: these
were to be / the seeds of men to come . . .*

—OVID, *THE METAMORPHOSES*

*. . . I can't make up / a name like Turnipseed! Or that /
I knew a man who went by such / a goodly name. . . .*

—MAURICE MANNING

I knew a man by such a name, though didn't know
       until you told me so, that a turnip seed is tiny,
a little bit of hardly anything. I should have known.
       Miniscule, a man, a goodly man, his seed—
what's that beside a war, misrule, history looming
       like a tower that throws its shadow
as it blocks the sun—the way (an old
       story) sin is cast on those most sinned
against, their coffins covered with a flag:
       stripes the backs of slaves way back when,
and stars—perhaps the last thing that you see
       when the landmine takes you—life and
limb, as the saying goes. My God. I knew a man,
       hardly more than a boy—he wasn't yet
out of his teens—a sweet guy name of Turnipseed,
       Carl as I recall, and I've always wondered how
the war turned out for him. Afraid, in fact, to know.

Showed up in class one day in uniform, but not
       to stay—to say goodbye—he seemed resigned,

a fatalist. Why struggle in a net that tightens
 when you fight its hold? Just say *so long*, and go.
All I could find to say was, please, take care
 of yourself. I mean, what good are words. *A little*
bit of hardly anything. And seeds?
 What good, as they said in 'Nam, if you
bought the farm—the field plowed with dragonseed,
 from which these fratricidal armies sprang
and fell upon each other's throats, and fell like dominoes,
 to join the ranks of headstones, *row on row on row* . . .
And Turnipseed? That seed was meant to grow.

AN ANSWERING MUSIC TO LINES
BY SAM HAMILL

Here I sit,
reading Prince Aki's chokra
in the Man'yoshu, wasting
my life on poetry, dreams
of spring rain . . .

Such a waste of glory, the *sakura* exuberant
       in spring, blossom crowding blossom . . . until
             the sky becomes one ruffled canopy of pink,
and for weeks the wind dismantles it, torn bits of
       blossom worry the air, the ground slowly buried in
             such sweet excess—a courtesan throwing
away, every day, a season's worth of silk . . .

To believe in poetry
is to believe the heart can be opened,
        and in the commerce of the heart,
thrift is ruin.

Rain, too, an abundance, recurrent cloud's
       refrain, drops unconcerned about their own
            redundance . . . spring's ground bass, its quiet
         insistence on memory's roof, refuge, *Kage-an*, shadow
house in the cedars, built by handiwork, long labor
       of love, like the poems—pure as artesian well water;
         the endless stream of books, the press
       you built from scratch, the begging bowl overflowing
with poems—Li Po, Tu Fu, Bashō, Issa, Yosano Akiko—
       you brought in like a tide to our insular world of letters . . .

. . . these tides

do not respect our work. And yet, to work
is the meaning of the tides and they steadily eat away
the memories of old labors we abandon . . .

old labors, the poetry of peace, abandoned and forever begun
            again, always a new war, fresh blood shines in the ditch, outrage
                        blossoms on its thorny stalk, as Death flatters the fools
who rule, makes them scythe his killing fields—
    (said Yeats: *why should old men not be mad?*)
            but look, how the nootka rose clings to the cliffs
                        where land drowns in the waves, the seawind
            tears at the petals, and the gulls scream . . .

This dead weight we carry
like an ancient grief is ours
because we will it—the lovely burden
of the verb **to be**
as it becomes attached . . .

As the wild rose holds with such tenacity
            the ledge, the waves so far below (such a long way
                        to fall)—a man is fighting his way through the brush,
            wanting to break free to the place where
the view opens out to the sea, and over there—the mountain,
            like an astonishment, rises above the clouds . . .

what's any mountain but a signpost
along a traveler's route?

Is this Odysseus, home after so many years?
            But his dog doesn't recognize him, his faithful
                        wife is wrapped in the shroud she was weaving,
and he is not the same man who set out in his youth, his scars
            notwithstanding, he has broken his sword, has sat in
                        the shrines of Kyoto, has found the Kannon

and foresworn violence, and by patient labors, become
        himself, a poet, a raker of sand:

Raking the sand, one sifts through illusions and deceits, through guilt and
embarrassment and anger, until, eventually, slowly and carefully raking
        the sand, one
gets at last to the sand.

As the moon turns the raked sand to a river, its silver
        a flow of light, a breeze enters the silence
without disturbing it, being itself made of silence . . .

In a single yard of silk, there is infinite space;
    Language is a deluge from one small corner of the heart.
Lu Chi, or you? And does it matter, really?
        Of Gary Snyder reciting Keats, you wrote: *Outside,*
the same moon rose above the water
that Wang Wei watches rise over the river
a thousand years before. It was the same night.
It was the same poem.
                For calling things by their right name,
                nine bows, Sam, nine bows.

ENDINGS, FROM A VERSE
BY GWENDOLYN BROOKS

WITH THANKS TO TERRANCE HAYES FOR THE MODEL

The duck fats rot in the roasting pan
And it's over and over and all,
The fine fraught smiles, and spites that began
Before it was over and all.

—FROM "THROWING OUT THE FLOWERS,"
ANNIE ALLEN

Such a long slow stream leads to the
place in the reeds where the duck
hides her eggs, thick shells sheltering the rich fats
within that feed the unborn, in the wet rot
that cushions the nest safely tucked in
the reeds like Moses in his basket in the
old story, boy about to be lifted into the roasting
sun, wrapped in Egyptian cotton—slow pan

across the ages, following the Nile, *now* and
then in a single frame, time's transit of its
long collective memory, a story told over
and over (the rescue, the turning against) and
the hawk swooping . . . it's about to be over
before the hatching, her useless flurry and
beating of wings—all her eggs broken—all

her pretty ones, undone. And the daughter of the
Pharaoh, God's pawn, lonely in the stone halls, the fine
linens, the long sun-struck afternoons, fraught
with a girl's dreams, where the beguiling smiles

of the servants are as false as the promises and
prayers of the priests, plotting, filled with spites,
sealing the women alive in the tombs that
house the *fellahin*'s hope of another life. What began
                              before
in a different time, another place, echoes in the call: it
rose skyward among the cotton rows; it was
the oldest cry: *let my people go*, and before it was over,
(is it ever over?), promises broken like bodies, and
eggs—the hawks circling over and over us all.

TO THINK OF HOW COLD

Cold in the earth, and the deep snow piled above thee . . .
—EMILY BRONTË, "REMEMBRANCE"

To think of how cold in the earth—how cold
     to have let her bury him, wrong, wrong, wrong . . .
          wrong says the struck bell, the footsteps of bronze,
wrong says the path through echoing stones,
       wrong says the cypress, casting a long
         Tuscan shadow on Ohio ground, all wrong
to let him lie below the lawn where no one walks
     with a light step, or a lifted heart—no one,
       no one—the hawthorn trees are skeletal,
only the pines offer shelter to the silent wren,
     but the bird has forgotten everything, its song, even
       the shape of its nest, and the rest of it—
it paused too long on an angel of stone, only
     those marbled wings could bear the cold here;
       cold in the earth—imagine a room
carved from icy clay, roots dangling from its roof,
     feeding a tree that he cannot see
       from geometry's hollow under the snow,
and cold, so implacably cold. *Do not grow old*
     as I grew old, says the ghost of Lear, *for though*
       I am gone, and the stage grown dark,
I walk the heath and my mind conjures
     an end to this cold, a funeral pyre—and look! Cordelia
       coming at last, like a blazing torch,
in a heaven of heat and a roar of fire.

GNAWED BONE, COVERED BRIDGE

with thanks to Jynne Dilling Martin and Ross Leckie

Look how your imagined person sits close to the sea
on a driftwood log, foam damp on her toes, teeth skimming
the last scraps of meat off the bare frame of an albatross

where it had washed up, long since fallen from the neck
  of an ancient mariner, barely a boy when Coleridge
set him on the deck of that ill-fated ship, and, plagued

by his own guilt, made him shoot the albatross, all that
white majesty a mass of bloody feathers on the deck.
. . . *a melancholy thing,* Coleridge once wrote, *to see a man, like the Sun
in the close of the Lapland summer, meridional in his horizon . . .*

how long that winter's white was sure to last,
how near the fast approaching night, summer
a brief lit spell in the long dark surrounding it,

months where the sun was preserved only in jars
of fruit, aglow on the cellar shelves when the candle
flame, lifted, becomes a contagion of light. How long
has it been, scraping the bones of an ancient guilt, grinding
enamel on bone, white on white—

but listen: the sound of fingers on ivory,
        as the pianist, thirty years gone,
                        plays on in the digital eternity
of binary numbers, still bent over the keys,
                (right foot keeping time)
            Thelonious Monk, "Round Midnight," opens the night,

floods it with music, as the Gemini telescope on
        Mauna Kea fills the dark sky with a furious froth
of stars—so much fire out there
                it puts the Milky Way to shame.
    As the child, standing at noon with her mother in the cool shelter
of the covered bridge,
                    though she sees the blinding square
        of annihilating light at both ends of the dark passage,
and hears the troubled waters below, knows herself
        held in the blessed shade
                of the moment, and takes heart.

WRITING IN SAND WHILE WALKING IN WALT'S FOOTPRINTS

As I ebb'd with the ocean of life,
As I wended the shores I know,
As I walk'd where the ripples continually wash . . .

—WALT WHITMAN

Walking the shores with Whitman, under the dimming
stars of the eastern dawn, a small dog at our heels,
the dog's mind mostly in his nose, reeling in the scents
of a half-rotted fish, damp sand, a lost sandal, a beached
jellyfish—he yips, and draws back: a translucent medusa
with a paralyzing sting, a rider of currents, thrown off
by its parents, a generation fixed to the reef: freed,
a gelatinous bell dangling a fringe of arms, boneless,
only the ocean holds it together;

                                    left by the tide, as it
ebb'd with the ocean of life, helpless, it finally dries
on the shore, only a little venom left to burn-
ish the nose of a dog, walking at the heels of an old
poet, who, with a toe, writes a word in the sand,
and the tide, a last flourish of foam, answers in kind.

III Lifelines

BIRD'S-EYE VIEW, CLOSE-UP, A RETROSPECTIVE

The egg had been a long time hatching.
    Forced to sit there, sun up sun down, unmoving, a decoy
       of yourself—only the soothing feel of the cool
          shell on your hot breast, the nothing to do, the fear of snakes,
      the readied beak, the hawk in the back of your mind.
The nest had been months in the making.
      The gathering arduous, drawing the strands
        of hair, the bits of fur caught in the brambles.
          the stalks of straw almost too large for the beak,
     and then the weaving, the intricate insertions and
        the pull out toward the light again.
The mate had been a hard road finding, all the ways it could be
     wrong, so many all fluff and feathers, strutting
        their stuff and gone with the first furious peck,
    and then the hunter's gun that took the one
        that *was* the one, and sent him to the waiting mouths
       of dogs, and then the rain, the rain, and then
         the need to dance the dance again.
The migration had been miles on the wing, above the curving shore
     where the pounding surf was your truest guide, and the white froth
      of the breaking waves, and the strange pull
        from the center of your mind that said north,
    and north and north, and the high crying of the flock around you,
      the changing light, your wings spread wide, and always the
      wind,
        the wind you could fight, or ride, soaring toward
       summer.
The first flight had not been easy, the nest walls growing closer every day,
     the open beak no longer fed, the other chick kept pushing you
      to the edge: that endless drop below the nest . . .

At the start, all dark it was, and solid overhead,
>> the same below, walled in with nothing but the pulsing sound:
>>> ka dum, ka dum, ka dum . . . the slowing beat . . .
>>> the fearsome sound of cracking . . .
The egg took forever hatching.

WHAT THE KITE SEES

The line is out, the long light plays along
my sides, paper—all of me—but shaped so perfectly
for catching wind.
                            And if I'm held in childish hands,
it matters not a whit to me, for I have the master view,
the long perspective of the airborne one
who floats above the scene . . . I pass
through clouds without a trace
or touch; from down there, you, the ones
who run with me—you only dream you fly
by the extension of a length of twine;
                            how small you look from here—
while I am high on air, so cool at this sweet altitude,
and yours but a playtime world—toy cars and model houses
on a game board far below, meaningless and
mean, and I, the paper wonder of the world: bow down
before my streaming majesty! I see you there
the way a god looks down on ants, and smiles to see
how you scurry after crumbs, then puts a giant
thumb straight down—the power's in the distance, after all.

        The world is growing larger now, the line
I'd loved, reeled out to set me free,
is shortened more and more,
        and as it shrinks,
see how the earth
        comes up at me . . .
    without the long,
the lovely line,
I'm just torn

paper
in the grass,
and the wind is
finished with me.

INTIMATIONS

While bent grass covers our footfalls
    like all things that whisper and sift—
the sound of a long silk skirt as it slips
    around a corner, the sweet spill
of water on a mossy rock, the thick
    carpet of green drinking back the splash—
all things merely hinted—felt but uncertain:

as if entering the half-lit halls of a dream,
    something is moving slow under cover, alive,
like a diver's light under water at night:
    something between sound and sight,
what the men—sitting under the Arctic stars,
    around the hole they have cut in the ice—await;
their long lines, life lines, attached to the one
    who swims below layers of ice, in silence,
except for the regular hiss of his own
    breathing device, and, as the heavens spin
above us, and the hours pass, we wait
    for that pull on the line that says
the diver is there, wanting to break through
    to the air, carrying whatever it was that had
so long lain below, in the soundless depths,

that, for years, every muffled sound had suggested,
    every soft footfall seemed to approach, every
whisper of silk when the wind stirred the curtains—

intimations about to be substance, as the light
    from below grew closer and brighter, the diver,

safe on the long line, about to breach
  the surface tension of the sea, his outline
clearing, and something clutched in his glove,
  something we all leaned forward, straining
(through the clouds of our own breath
    in the wintry air) to see.

MOONLIT WAKE

The broken moonpath on the darkened sea, churned
    by the blades of passing boats,
                the drowning sound
of what fell from the sloping decks
                and slipped into oblivion,
like all that was crucial, momentous, cost
    so many ruined lives, back when—
                now, what was that?
the *what* that once meant everything.

Below, on the black silk of the tide
    the moon has spread her silver,
            and the silent shapes slide by;
the motors churn,
            the surface torn—below,
the manatees, unconscious of the blades' approach,
    the sleeping village where the drones fly low,
life too unsuspecting, slow,
            for the speed at which
the mindless motors go. The moon
            is what remains.
This light that makes a path across the sea.
    So pretty, and the path,
            a trick of light, unreal.

What stays is what amazes. What is that? What hurts,
    and soon will not;
            the moon will turn its face away.

But not for long.
   The cycle means return, another
  bloody crop,
   and those who were not there,
who just arrived, will hope,
    as we once did,
     to make it stop.

SHELLS

It was the old names we thought
to erase by writing—rising
from the page in their place,
      bodies too lively for words,
carrying, like fireflies, their own light,
windborne, something unerring,
hollow as the shaft of feathers,
whose vanes help an arrow go straight
to the fault in the rock, the place where
water is waiting to pour
      like song from a hidden spring—
            yes, it was names
we feared most of all, we who had lived in them
like hermit crabs in borrowed shells,
walking sideways across the endless dunes,
soft underbellies hidden, bearing
their need on their backs, feeling
for waves to return them to sea,
the waves receding before them, exposing
(it didn't matter which way you looked) the sand,
and above it, the heavens, a name to harden the blue.
And soon, outgrowing an armor only adopted,
always naked again and searching (or be crushed
by the walls that once meant safety) . . .
          but what did it mean
to shed, again and again, the shells—
to write up a storm, sweeping everything
clean, ending like Beethoven's Sixth
in a sweet *allegretto*, and a coda
of peace (*pianissimo*), and when it was done

nothing was changed but the page, not
a stalk of grass disturbed . . .
                    yet, didn't we leave
the beach littered with beautiful shells, outgrown
shelters from which life had moved on, gleaming
among the cases of the still unexploded
munitions, the tides turning again,
a silent sky invaded by thunder,
the peace after storm forever expected.

UNMOVED

Made when the mountain grew quiet again,
and the lava stopped, mid-flow—
after the tongues of molten lava, and fire below,
    had swallowed the road, the little homes, and time
        had passed, impassive, slow, and, unrelenting,
solidified these great blank sloping
    fields of shining black, just so
the interrupted past remains, a hardened script
    in which, now, bits of green insert themselves
        and force the stony ground to part
            as if the ground itself contained some fresh idea
of what it might become, some bright obliteration
of what had passed: as if a train, crossing an old terrain,
    could stop, open its doors, and pouring out
        of its lighted cars . . .
                but no, the darkness of a time
that's gone has swallowed them back—
lost again, trapped in implacable fact, escaping
    nothing but injured memory's doomed attempt
    at alteration.
           Tonight reclaimed its hold,
and the moon rose, leaving a line like the trail
    of a finger dipped in silver on the solid lava fields,
        the darkened scene, the small tendril of green
        reaching for tomorrow's sun.

FOR THE FIRST TIME

Nothing in the pond prepared him
      for this—not the flashy time
as a tadpole; not the amazing day his tail,
      absorbed, stretched into legs
that let him safely leap from harm;
      not the somnolent lapse
of winter—though he recalled the thunder
      of the ice that broke above him,
woke him where he slept, suspended
      inside winter like a pearl in a shell,
Spring the sound of cracking in his luminous
      half-sleep: but now—the bells!

When the first bells sounded in
      in the air, unaccustomed to their peal,
its power and reach, its slow decay,
      unable to account for it—the frog's
astonishment was half alarm. What
      had he heard? And he but half-awake,
just come from deep within
      the pond, where he had breathed
the oxygen cold water carries
      through his skin, and sunk in slumber
there, survived, close to frozen,
      submarine and blind, through all
the months of silence, and of snow.
      And now—the bells!

Imagine that: to wake in such a way,
from such a depth, to Spring, and to the ringing

of the bells—but not as they had ever rung
before, to hear for the first time:

                              it would be that day
the wars ended, when all the towers rang
their bells, the air was one reverberant
sound: as if we, too, had, dormant, lived
in some dark depths, cold-blooded,
ears stopped, our eyes glued shut,
ice crystals formed
around the heart, but now
(permit a poet's dream)—the bells!

BEFORE OUR EYES

the one who has fallen:
bird with beak wide open.
dog rigid on the kitchen floor.
naked fledgling on the sidewalk
below the useless nest. Or the star-
fish left by the tide's withdrawal, still
breathing through its tubal arms but not
for long; even so, the slug making its slow
way across the paving in a drought will never
reach the damp for which, in sluggish thoughts, it
lusts. And woe to the sloth who moves so syrupy slow,
who can't escape the fast approaching walls of roaring fire.
All the fallen, and then the million leaves, and it is fall, and we
are sore afraid. For now the falling has come to our block, to our
neighborhood, the sound of splintering wood, of gun rounds spraying
bullets everywhere. Nowhere to hide, and even the longest line must reach
the limits of the page, and age takes its toll, and what was sure must fail, and fall.

But then, as when a ball of yarn is wound up from the long unravel of a failed
attempt to knit, the pattern lost, the knitter on to other things, or when
the great thread in the hero's hand be slowly gathered in, and he
return through the high walls of labyrinth to the sunlit mouth
or the leaves of autumn be raked and piled, and set to burn,
the ashes at rest in the urn, or the small boat unwind
the anchor rope and lift it to the stern, the boat
raise its small sail, the sailor holding the line
that sets the sheet to the wind, the tiller
firm in her hand, the wind rising,
the little craft heading into
the rising sun, the sheen
on the sea a shield
against the dark,
even a dinghy
can be an
ark, day
in, day
out.

THE USES OF WHAT IS HOLLOW

A hollow time—*how with this rage*
shall beauty hold a plea, how look
within ourselves, our commonwealth,
without those leering faces looking back,
the ones that Brueghel caught in oil and fixative:
dim eyes, mouths gaping, wet with pleasure
at the painful execution of a god—the lynch mobs
of history, whose shadow marks the hollow,
the emblem of the tree itself disgraced.

el condor pasa . . . can you hear that haunting sound, uncanny
in its beauty, panpipes of Peru that mime the sound of wind,
the spread of wings, the soaring beauty of the condor high
above the Andes, glory in the pass—*and, when Pan*
thought he had captured her, he held instead
only the tall marsh reeds . . . and made of hollow loss
a song, and of the vulture's circle overhead, such music
that every reed could sing when given breath,
pure melody born of wind and emptiness.
so piercing and so high, *el condor pasa* overhead . . .
look up: no, higher! do you see him now? His wings outspread,
the **V** that children draw when they mean *bird* and *far*
and *sky*, the condor gives the emptiness its size,
in search of death
on which it feeds, and as it flies, the panpipes
play—the music is so lovely, it could stop the breath.

ARS POETICA, 2017

to grasp, like Prometheus, the fire—without
the power to give it away . . .

—BETTY ADCOCK

At first a silhouette on the horizon. Then
turning solid, like Schiller coming up the path to meet
the adorable sisters, and they, pretending not to watch,
         their hearts, all the time, pounding,
      driven by the same spring force (that would
tear them apart), the same force that drives
the salmon upriver, against the current, the odds,
     back to the home pool, even as
        the autumn mind, in spite of itself,
turns backward, with the same feverish glow as autumn
gives the summer's leaves, a deceptive glamour,
warming the past with an amber light, like brandy
held up to the fire, or the sun sinking at dusk
        into the water, into the Baltic Sea
     each night, where, in the mythical depths
of Lithuanian folktale, lies the amber castle
of the female sun, burning in the dark water,
a globe the color of harvest, aglow
there in the depths of the past, though
     the amber, congealed sap of a once
living force, is broken into bits, and the mythic
castle with it—strung now as beads, and hung,
a charm, around the neck of a daughter,
     like the one in a Greek dream, picking flowers
        when the earth opened,

and in a swirl of violet cape and the pounding of hoofs,
the dark god broke out of the earth
driven by the same spring force, consequential
and mortal,

         and up there, hanging over the mythic
fields of what recurs and recurs (though never the same,
and never to be reconciled)—what is that?

                   A hot air balloon filled
with passengers who paid to be raised
in a basket, to be up there looking down on
the ground where they live, a place shrunken now
beneath their gaze, while their bloated shadow floats
like a jellyfish in a green sea, barely a smudge on the pastures below,
the trace of their passage less than a breath of smoke
from a coal-fired engine—a blast of tarnished air
from the actual past, heavy metal delivered from memory.

                 Useless to warn the girl, whose
hand will always be reaching out for the flowers, or
the sisters inflamed with Schiller, as he with the tricolor
dream of a world he could never inhabit . . .

             useless to comfort
the eyeless Tiresias who knew how terrible is
wisdom when it knows itself useless,

              and useless to read
the names on the shining black wall of the Vietnam
Memorial, the text of exactly what war has accomplished—

    And look, there, standing high above the tragic scene,
not the little figures of the wise ancients that Yeats saw
carved into the deep blue stone—but there, standing high
above Arlington, against the blank lapis of the sky:
a horse with the torso and head of a man, yes,
it is Chiron, the last of the hybrids, the sage and terribly wounded
centaur for whom immortality was a curse,

             and he gave it away

to Prometheus, who stole the god's fire and gave it away,
as art gives the power to give it away,
for that fire is the gift that cannot be held,
for it will burn to an ash those (born
and born again, war without end) who would hold it.

LISTEN

The mind is made out of the animals
it has attended.

—ROBERT BRINGHURST

A marmot by the side
of the road, eyes enormous, a long
thought flaring out of them, lighting
the embers you hadn't known
still smoldered, and listen! the marmot
raises his whistle of alarm,

                              the embers
flame up, blue at their core, rising
until they are the blue feathers of the jay,
noisy in the branches of the ancient
bristlecone pine, twisted and gnarled
by time, and wise to us, high

                              above the stream
muttering to itself among the cattails,
the reeds erupting in frogs, green and angry
at what has happened to the water, the foul
way it has begun to refuse their company,
   and look—

                  unfurling in the stony shallows,
   snails, unwinding, as if their shells were being
      unmade, the spirals a slow unravel in
the dying of the light, twilight, blue as the heron
caught for a moment on the wing, held
in the eye:

                  the eye

                              for that second filled with

wings, the ear with their beating on the wind,
the air a fan of blue feathers opening
                    like the great eye of the sun
as it took a last burning look at us, and slid
with a green flash under the horizon,
into morning on the other side of the world.

And it was then the fish,
                    having refused the hook,
slid off among the weeds, alive
in the dark waters of night, playing among
the confetti of moonlight, bright bits
tossed in the ripples of water, and its body
said *rest*, said *slide with the slow tide*
of the currents,
                    said only its own motion,
the slow swing of the earth among stars,
the slow burn of the stars among
stars, the recurrence of things that are
never the same, like those
    that return from a long journey
in the clothes of another tribe, dreaming
their dreams,
                    as someone who has lived
a long time in a strange country returns,
and only the silence is there
to receive her,
                    that, and the dog
who has lain at the portal, who rises,
and from his throat comes a howl, a cry
pulled like taffy—*that* sweet, *that*
extended, *that* endlessly supple, that
animal greeting—
                    and, as we break through
the mirror, the ancient cry rises,
full-throated, our own.

FROM
TOURIST IN HELL (2010)

HISTORY AS CRESCENT MOON

The horns
    of a bull
      who was placed
before a mirror at the beginning
       of human time;
        in his fury
at the challenge of his double,
         he has, from
          that time to this,
been throwing himself against
         the mirror, until
       by now it is
shivered into millions of pieces—
         here an eye, there
        a hoof or a tuft
of hair; here a small wet shard made
         entirely of tears.
And up there, below the spilt milk of
       the stars, one
      silver splinter—
parenthesis at the close of a long sentence,
     new crescent,
    beside it, red
   asterisk of
  Mars
   *

MAGNIFICAT

When he had suckled there, he began
to grow: first, he was an infant in her arms,
but soon, drinking and drinking at the sweet
milk she could not keep from filling her,
from pouring into his ravenous mouth,
and filling again, miraculous pitcher, mercy
feeding its own extinction . . . soon he was
huge, towering above her, the landscape,
his shadow stealing the color from the fields,
even the flowers going gray. And they came
like ants, one behind the next, to worship
him—huge as he was, and hungry; it was
his hunger they admired most of all.
So they brought him slaughtered beasts:
goats, oxen, bulls, and finally, their own
kin whose hunger was a kind of shame
to them, a shrinkage; even as his was
beautiful to them, magnified, magnificent.

The day came when they had nothing left
to offer him, having denuded themselves
of all in order to enlarge him, in whose
shadow they dreamed of light, and that
is when the thought began to move, small
at first, a whisper, then a buzz, and finally,
it broke out into words, so loud they thought
it must be prophecy: they would kill him,
and all they had lost in his name would return,
renewed and fresh with the dew of morning.
Hope fed their rage, sharpened their weapons.

And who is she, hooded figure, mourner now
at the fate of what she fed? And the slow rain,
which never ends, who is the father of that?
And who are we to speak, as if the world
were our diorama—its little figures moved
by hidden gears, precious in miniature, tin soldiers,
spears the size of pins, perfect replicas, history
under glass, dusty, old-fashioned, a curiosity
that no one any longer wants to see,
excited as they are by the new giant, who feeds
on air, grows daily on radio waves, in cyberspace,
who sows darkness like a desert storm,
who blows like a wind through the boardrooms,
who touches the hills, and they smoke.

IN A TIME OF WAR

Flies, caught in the sap of the living
tree, some day will be
precious, dressed in amber—just so
the past appears to the present, gem-
like in its perfect preservation,
the hardened gold of yesterday, a relic
through which today's sun shines.

But those who are caught in the sticky
sap of actual time, insects in the odds
against them, who struggle in the ooze,
slowly sink into the mass,
the numberless, anonymous dead . . .
till the atrocious becomes
the mundane, our senses numb
from the sheer litany of repetition . . .

let us, then, just watch this one small
desperate fly, stuck first by the feet,
and then, in its struggles, entangled
entirely in the glob of sap, its wings
heavy as a brass angel's, until it is
all at once still, a dark speck
in a bubble of sap
oozing from the felled tree
in a forest marked for the mill.

How many millennia will pass
before a tear-drop lavaliere of amber
carrying its cargo of loss

will adorn the vanity of another
creature, the fly a fossil of a species
no longer present on the Earth,
the Earth itself a speck in a cosmos where
galaxies are carded like cotton on a comb
and pulled out into a distance
where some new fabric is being spun
and shimmers in the firelight
of countless, burning suns.

THE SHOW MUST GO ON

I just want to remember
the dead piled high behind the curtain.

—MAHMOUD DARWISH

The play had been staged as long as we could remember,
a sordid drama in which truth kept changing sides,
the name of the enemy was never the same;

sometimes the players poured over the edge
of the proscenium, spilling into the audience,
who ran terrified from the house

that had become a scene of massacre; sometimes
the drama played at a distance relaxingly remote,
caught and burnished in the bright little

dollhouse screen, so far away it was no more
than fireflies in a bottle, mere hiccups of light—
the carpet bombing, the village torched.

So that—unless the street were yours,
and the terrible crying of the wounded
your own—it was impossible

to tell what was real, so much was not
what it seemed, was simply *not:*
not at all, not any more, not this, not that—

yet the music was upbeat, the messenger
smiling, the voiceover a reassuring pour
of syrup in the artificial light. Meanwhile,

though the labels changed, and the set
was rearranged for every act—the plot
remained unvarying, never veering off

from the foretold end. So, when the curtain falls,
we know for certain what is going to be
piled high behind it. Yet we wait, we go on

waiting, as if the bodies might still move,
the actors untwine themselves from the pile,
step through the opening of the folded-back curtain

into the brightly lit house, the resounding applause,
the audience pulling on coats to go home,
silent streets filling again with laughter and talk;

while deep within the darkened hall, the actors,
by their lit mirrors, lift from their sweat-soaked
faces, the eyeless masks.

ESTABLISHMENT

Death had established himself in the Red Room,
the White House having become his natural
abode: chalk-white façade, pillars like the bones
of extinct empires, armed men crawling its halls
or looking down, with suspicion, from its roof;
its immense luxury, thick carpets, its plush velvet chairs—
all this made Death comfortable, bony as he is, a fact
you'd barely notice, his camouflage a veil of flesh
drawn over him, his tailor so adroit, and he so elegant,
so *GQ*, almost a dandy, so suited for the tables
where the crystal, silverware, the swans of ice gleamed
with the polished purity of light on precious things;
Death was the guest of honor here, confiding, convivial
among friends who leaned to light his cigar—his power
seemed their own, body counts at their command;
a power beyond even their boy-wet dreams
was now a custom they feared to lose: each saw
the world the way a hooded falcon on the fist
sees it, blind, waiting for the next release; one word
could bury villages alive, could send
battalions to an early grave—

                         so Death can rest
assured, smiling at such a harvest—and so
deliciously unseasonable, like berries in winter.
Welcome houseguest, he stretches his ancient
frame, warm under expensive wool, sipping wine,
picking his teeth with a last bone,
meat all the sweeter for being
the lambs of honor, corn-fed and unsuspecting;
or the children playing in the rubble

who reach down for a souvenir of steel
that has fallen from the sky—really,
Death has seldom had a better season or such
a winning score; he must see to their protection,
these little men who think to be *his* master—
flatter a fool and make him useful, he thinks,
and smiles benignly, whitely, at his hosts,
assuring them of his gratitude, his presence
at their councils, his everlasting support . . .
until, no longer able to hide
his triumph, his delight, forgetting the flesh
he has clothed himself in for the occasion,
he rubs his hands together
in the ancient gesture of satisfaction,
naked bone on bone—how the sound grates,
how the grateful sparks fly!

SATURDAY NIGHT

Moonlit rocks, sand, and a web of shadows,
     thrown over the world from the cottonwoods,
        the manzanita, the ocotillo; it is
the hour of the tarantula, a rising
     as predictable as tide, irritable as
        moon drag. And if this were
a sci-fi film, the spider would be
     huge as a water tank, it would loom
        red-eyed and horrible, its mandibles
wet with drool or blood, and screams
     would be heard as it stumbled
        through the cactus and the brush,
trees upended, small bodies
     crunching in its path; in the distance,
        police cars, lights flashing, sirens blaring,
would be tearing down the highways,
     dust rising in their wake, and cars
        would begin streaming from distant
cities, the terror growing with each
     report of it—the creature, like a figure
        from the bad conscience of the race,
hungry, hairy, would be coming
     for every blonde, she, hiding in a million
        bedrooms, breasts heaving under
filmy white lace . . . but now as the film
     runs down, in a rush of stale air
        the hydraulic spider deflates, the saline
leaks from the implants of the bed-
     room blonde, the moon's projection
        clicks off, and the night is as it was,

a place where fear takes its many
        forms, and the warships gather in
                a distant gulf, where a small man
with more arms than a Hindu god
        has set a desert alight, and grief blooms;
                while here, the theaters are full
of horror on the screen, and you can hear—
            over the sinister canned music,
                    the chainsaws, and the screams—
the sound of Coke sucked up through straws,
            your own jaws moving as you chew.

ENCOUNTER IN THE LOCAL PUB

*Unlike Francis Bacon, we no longer believe
in the little patterns we make of the chaos of history.*
—OVERHEARD REMARK

As he looked up from his glass, its quickly melting ice,
into the bisected glowing demonic eyes of the goat,
he sensed that something fundamental had shifted,

or was done. As if, after a life of enchantment, he
had awakened, like Bottom, wearing the ears of an ass,
and the only light was a lanthorn, an ersatz moon.

It was not that the calendar hadn't numbered the days
with an orbital accuracy, its calculations
exact, but like a man who wants to hang a hammock

in his yard, to let its bright net cradle him, but only
has one tree, so he—wild and aware of it—knew
he had lost the order he required, and with it, rest—

his thoughts only a sagging bundle of loose ends,
and the heart, a naked animal in search of a pelt,
that once fell for every Large Meaning it could

wrap itself in, as organs are packed in ice for transit
from one ending to the next, an afterlife of parts—and
the whole? Exorbitant claim—not less than all,

and oddly spelled; its ear rhyme is its opposite,
the great hole in the heart of things. The goat,
he noticed, had a rank smell, feral. Unnerved,

he looks away, watches the last of his ice
as it melts, the way some godlike eye might see
the mighty glaciers in a slow dissolve back into sea.

He notes how incommensurate the simile, a last
attempt to dignify his shaking gaze, and reaches
for the bill; he's damned if the goat will pay.

WHAT LOVES, TAKES AWAY

If the nose of the pig in the market of Firenze
has lost its matte patina, and shines, brassy,
even in the half-light; if the mosaic saint
on the tiles of the Basilica floor is nearly gone,
worn by the gravity of solid soles, the passing
of piety; if the arms of Venus have re-entered
the rubble, taken by time, her perennial lover,
mutilating even the memory of beauty;

                                  and if

the mother, hiding with her child from
the death squads closing in,
if she, trying to keep the child
quiet, to keep them from being found out,
holds her hand over his mouth, holds him
against her, tighter and tighter, until he stops
breathing;

                if the restorer—trying to bring back
to perfection the masterpiece scarred by its
transit through time, wipes away,
by mistake, the mysterious smile . . .

                              if what

loves, and love is, takes away what it aims
to preserve,

              then here is the place to fall
silent, meaning well but in danger
of marring what we would praise, unable
to do more than wear down the marble
steps to the altar, smother the fire
we would keep from the wind's extinction,

                          or if, afraid

of our fear, we lift the lid from the embers, and send
abroad, into the parched night, a flight of sparks,
incendiary, dying to catch somewhere,
hungry for fuel, the past, its dry provision
tinder for brilliance and heat, prelude
to cold, and to ash . . .

VOICES FROM THE LABYRINTH

MINOS

lean close I am only the echo of a voice
husk of power king of cobwebs cast off shell of the cicada
the singing insect long since flown memory a spectral thread
broken line across the centuries perforations
a place to tear open again the rift in time string of tears
the clew that led from one room of the dream to the next
became a flame burning along a fuse until
it lit the black night of the Aegean
gone our port of pleasure there pause again at the word
pleasure
the way wind lingers in bright air
turns hot Sirocco stirs the nerves again blows the dry earth
Ariadne in a dress of dust grows indistinct
(no, stay a moment . . . I want to know . . .)
the dolphin leaps only on the peeling blue of the painted wall
a lizard brushes my foot Theseus only a name
for the passage of power from one place to another
we were lovers of peace of art the winding measures of dance
of poems yes we were liars always new gods
thirsty for blood swallow the old I am tired
where are the vineyards the arbors
they say the way in is the way out we end
at the place of beginning black sails for the old kings
white in the hold for the next

ARIADNE

They say
I placed the clew
in his hand (even my father shamed came to believe it)

but it was their story told long after what happened
left us beggars in our once rich island
before the earth erupted before the sea rose
we were a city without walls our complications
were within artists traders worshippers
of the changing moon
we were ourselves the labyrinth
and the clew I was she who served the Lady
who wears the crescent holds the twin serpents
who is the reel
around which the thread is wound
now even the olive trees nothing but pillars of smoke
and I standing among ruins
looked up into the eyes of Greece
fierce bearers of spears gods of sun and thunder
carrying shields on which
we were history merely
an old dream of peace
the white bull
grazing in the wild grass
the cows deep
in perpetual
summer
the ibex abroad in the mountain
in the field poppies aflame like red silks
gone in the fiery night
the past only a painting crumbling from the walls
and I a figment now
a shade who flits
along the labyrinth of time
history twisted like a skein of yarn
back on the spindle
back to the spinner's hand
I run my hand along but where is the wall
where is the world
(what have they done to my brother)

of course we went mad   when they came
there was so much death
they seemed   almost its master
Daedalus   serves a new god
and I   a foreign figure
in a Greek story
the Greek key is a maze
it is *their* design   fit
for the walls of their temples of stone
finding us weak
they took what they say we gave
I shall free myself
from that fiction
as soon   as I find
the right turn
a way out
of these
lines

DAEDALUS

always there are questions   always   answers disagree
like quarrelsome neighbors   who argue about everything
where the fence goes   who owns the fig tree   whose god made
the world green   whose dog tore the garden up   whose story
is true   whose story is this we are in   I should know
I am Daedalus   artificer   artist   teller of tales   trapped
in the maze   of my own invention   Dante whirling
in the circles of an exile's hell   vile dreams   of monsters
the torture of my enemies   incendiary   I am   every exile
in my mind   ascending   living under   one lord after another
I am the ringmaster   the man on the merry-go-round horse
I am the architect who comes home to a ruined house
Marcel   who ends one thousand pages   with a man beginning to write
Finnegan's scribe   with the bad eyes   the many tongues
the wake   into which we sail   to begin again
born tired   the poet whose *way forward   is the way   back*

I Daedalus was hired to map the underground its twisted ways
keep it secret put the lid on a painted ceiling of stars
       still air extends itself sun dazzles the sea
         a handful of floating feathers marks the limits of art
Knossos drowns in sand again
               Gnosis down the bloody drain of history
and I only a man in search of an exit hired to construct it

MINOTAUR

      Do not mistake me I am not what you think
        what you think is polluted by what you were told
         if man is the measure then man is the monster
      See I have taken the long gold clew in my mouth
           I am reeling it in reeling it in
               a man is attached
Theseus an obsolete hero sent long ago this time
I have pulled the knife from the heart of the plot
  even as I pull the line that he holds in his hand
    and thinks it his own see I am drawing him
    closer and closer   I can smell his fear now
      the line he believed would lead him out is
        pulling him inexorably in   I never
        let go I was born under the sign of
          Taurus we hold on whatever
            we've got stays caught
          I am hauling and
            hauling
             until
              we
             are
          face to face
        you are looking
         into my eyes
         I into yours
      now you see who we are
         tangled in

the spiraling threads
that curl
round and round
the central
axis
of the double helix
along
the nucleotides
of creation
where the past
is always
with us
and always open
to change
I have met you here
because it is time
there is so much past
it is late
just time enough
for an exit

FROM
*THE GIRL WITH BEES
IN HER HAIR* (2004)

EVERYTHING IS STARTING

The snow is filthy now; it has been
drinking oil and soot and car exhausts
for days, and dogs have marked it
with their special brand of brilliant
yellow piss;
            for a week after it fell,
the snow stood in frozen horror
at the icy chill, and hardened
on the top, and then, today, the thaw:
now everything is starting
up again—
            the traffic flows, the place
where dogs pause, and sniff, becomes,
once more, invisible to us, and in
the gutters of our streets, a minor Nile
floods from the old drifts into the gasping
drains; even the sewers are jubilant
in the rush that foretells spring; the rats
dance along the pipes;
                on all the trees,
the buds push against the sealed bark,
as if against the tight containment
of the past,
            while deep in the Florida Keys,
along some slow canal, the manatees roll
heavily in the dark stream, the way that sleepers
slowly turn in dream, and the cranes look
up, unrolling their long necks, possessed
by restlessness just before

they fly . . .

        light-years away, beyond the veils
of the Milky Way, out at the red edge
of creation, where everything is
always starting: there—a memory
shifts and gathers itself once more:
a memory of the time (if time it can
be called) when all that is the matter
or all that matter is, is drawn into
one place, as if into a single thought,
and (unimaginable) ignites,
shattering the ageless night in which
the cosmos only dreamed,
and in the oldest memory

                (of which I think
we have a share)
it was the endlessly unfolding flower
of fire—the rose of light that Dante
saw, its afterimage in the soul.
And from that flower, the seeds
of all the galaxies were
sown . . .

        now, in our own, the snow recedes,
the buds will shatter the end
of every twig, as everything is
starting up again, the crocus pokes
its purple, furled, above the thawing
ground,

        and when the local ember
of that first fiery bloom, our sun, touches
its silk with light, it will unfurl,
in perfect silence—unlike us,
who never were the point,
but still delight in being
the sole narrators, upstarts of the dawn.

FIELD OF VISION

And if the bee, half-drunk
on the nectar of the columbine,
could think of the dying queen, the buzz
of chaos in the hive, the agitation
of the workers in their cells, the veiled
figure come again to rob the combs—
then would the summer fields
grow still, the hum of propagation
cease, the flowers spread
bright petals to no avail—as if
a plug were drawn from a socket
in the sun, the light that flowed into
the growing field would fail;
for how should the bee make honey, then,
afraid to look, afraid to look away?

WHAT NARCISSUS GAVE THE LAKE

Write what you know. *And go on knowing only what
we know? And never know the lakeness of the lake?*

—CONSTANCE MERRITT

The lake loves what it sees, and what it sees
     is not what he saw, the beautiful boy in
the myth—for him, the water was pure reflection,
     his eyes greedily gathering back the face
that featured this image of himself, so famous
     a fixation, flypaper to the soul, saying nothing,
holding him fast on the lake's margin.
     The lake loves him differently, darkly,
looking up and out of its own depths,
     seeing him as a path of filtered light, a sounding
line through thick green weeds that lift and sway
     their slender length through the clouds of rising
silt, dark currents from the breeze above and
     from the springs that feed it underground;
the lake watches as the bright egg of his face wavers
     and breaks, shattering into bits and liquid
shards of light; at other times his face is jeweled
     by the brilliant fish who swim in rippling silver
schools—or mud erupts, frogs leap and break
     the surface tension on which his image rests,
and all at once, the man himself appears: a flash
     of solid flesh against a radiant, distant blue;
the water closes back. The lake sees through Narcissus
     the abundant life of its own being—for
had it not, that morning, raised its gaze
     to what, along its verge, was bent on self-regard,

it wouldn't know, as it knows now,
　　　　what multitudes it can contain,
would not have seen how its own dark currents
　　　　flow, nor known so many bright and darting
lives. The shifting likeness of all this was given
　　　　to the lake, in the contemplation of
that beautiful and beauty-blinded face.

MOON GATHERING

And they will gather by the well,
its dark water a mirror to catch whatever
stars slide by in the slow precession of
the skies, the tilting dome of time,
over all, a light mist like a scrim,
and here and there some clouds
that will open at the last and let
the moon shine through; it will be
at the wheel's turning when
three zeros stand like pawprints
in the snow; it will be a crescent
moon, and it will shine up from
the dark water like a silver hook
without a fish—until, leaning closer,
swimming up from the well, something
dark but glowing, animate, like live coals—
it is our own eyes staring up at us,
as the moon sets its hook,
as Artemis once drew her bow;
and they, whose dim shapes are no more
than what we will become, take up
their long-handled dippers
of brass, and one by one, they catch
the moon in the cup-shaped bowls,
and they raise its floating light
to their lips, and with it, they drink back
our eyes, burning with desire to see
into the gullet of night: each one
dips and drinks, and dips, and drinks,
until there is only dark water,
until there is only the dark.

"DON'T LOOK SO SCARED. YOU'RE ALIVE!"

for Marilyn Krysl

Who speaks? Now that the Muses
have traded their togas for faded rags,
now that their spring has dried up,
their once firm breasts old dugs sagging,
their thoughts wandering into clouds
of theory, inspiration's exhaust—who
is it then wakes the writer in the night
and speaks? Now that Clear Channel
has bought up the air and fills it with
babble and gas, and Truth lies
choking in a shuttered room; now
that the Angel with the flaming sword
has put the Garden to the torch—among
shards of bone, broken tablets, a mosaic
of haphazard art, the hyenas gather,
and the tanks roll on, and the homeland
crowds cheer on cue *(the dim boy
claps because the others clap)*—

Who sings to the dying, who wraps
in her shawl the charred lexicon left
on the steps of the ruined library
next to the toppled stone lion—
who turns away in contempt
from the limousine's passing,
Folly's regent, God's shadow
behind tinted, bullet-proof glass—

Who won't turn the page
to a grave for the language,
nor splinter the syntax to mimic
explosion, nor dismember sense
to appeal to sensation; who, knowing
the cliff face, the handholds, the rope,
reckless, swings out past the edge
in a wide, daring arc—the wind
there is howling, but her feet
find the ledge.

THIS STRAW AND MANURE WORLD

And the mare kicks at her traces, pulling the old-fashioned rig
       around Independence Hall, surrounded now by cheap aluminum
stands, fences to hold off terrorists, another fool's errand on which
       Smoky the Bear and his brethren, with their self-important official hats,
have been sent: the terrorists don't give a damn about our little historic
       pile of bricks and sentiment, from a time before empire, when
18th-century men, in what was hopefully called The Enlightenment, made
       their stand for autonomy, more economic than ideal, but sanctified by time
and by an empire's need for roots with some morality clinging to them—
       not just dirt. There was a prediction, back in Franklin's time, that if
the population grew at the current rate, the amount of horse manure
       would be, in another century, 18 feet deep. They weren't entirely wrong.
Though they didn't factor in the steam engine, Henry Ford, or the trolley car,
       they guessed right on the depth of horseshit, though most of it is in D.C.,
our new, Imperial capital: where the Washington Monument, white towering obelisk,
       glowers with its red electric eyes, a Klansman in a white hood,
staring down the blossoming Mall, admiring its reflection in the monumental pool.

JUST SO STORY

Do not make treaties with these people

—TRANSLATION OF NAVAJO MESSAGE INSCRIBED
ON THE DISK LEFT ON THE MOON BY NASA

It is very quiet on the moon. A cat squarls—
but that is back on earth, on streets of stone
where sound echoes: trashcans tipped over,
glass breaking, fear in a gray overcoat firing its
guns; it is all metal on metal—a plumber's snake
trying to shed its iron skin, clanking, sparks
flying; a steel beak hatching out of an egg
of glass, the cracking shell a shatter of ice
in the ear. While on the moon, an airless peace:
the craters aglow with distant sun, and nothing
to disturb the quiet dust.
                              In a grove deep in the past,
when the ibex was still bidden by its image drawn
with a stick in the sand—a lion came down to drink
where the moon lay, white and naked, on the pond,
trails of light around her, a corona of snakes.
The lion was very thirsty, and it drank and drank,
until the pond was dry, and the moon the barest
glimmer on the mud. And that is how darkness
first escaped from the place it had lain
on the bottom of the pond.
                              Now, the blood
from the kill no longer returns to the gods
so nothing is lost, but spills
in the road for the jackals to drink.
In the silence of the moon, Old Glory forever

flies in its fixed imitation of a flag in wind,
a permanent wave that can't disappoint
the eager cameras of the press by hanging limp
in the airless atmosphere of conquered space.

Far below, the busy cameras snap the photo-op:
a President, drawing his brows together
in the fixed imitation of a mind at work.
Down all the streets nearby, the wind rips
at the trash, you can hear the sound of
shredders in the shuttered rooms. Dogs bark.
The subway shakes the sidewalk grates.
Everywhere, the dark ascends
by stairs, by escalators, up through manholes
with their covers pushed away. Even by day,
though just a bit more slowly, the dark extends
its sway. The rats are growing bolder now;
you can hear the steady sound of gnawing
where they have dragged the last bright crust
of moon into their hole.

FOUND IN THE FREE LIBRARY

Write as if you lived in an occupied country.
—EDWIN ROLFE

And we were made afraid, and being afraid
we made him bigger than he was, a little man
and ignorant, wrapped like a vase of glass
in bubble wrap all his life, who never felt
a single lurch or bump, carried over
the rough surface of other lives like
the spoiled children of the sultans of old
in sedan chairs, on the backs of slaves,
the gold curtains on the chair
pulled shut against the dust and shit
of the road on which the people walked,
over whose heads he rode, no more aware
than a wave that rattles pebbles on a beach.

And being afraid we forgot to see
who pulled his golden strings—how
their banks overflowed while
the public coffers emptied, how
they stole our pensions, poured their smoke
into our lungs, how they beat our ploughshares
into swords, sold power to the lords of oil,
closed their fists to crush the children
of Iraq, took the future from our failing grasp
into their hoards, ignored our votes,
broke our treaties with the world,
and when our hungry children cried, the doctors
drugged them so they wouldn't fuss,

and prisons swelled enormously to hold
the desperate sons and daughters of the poor.
To us, they just said war, and war, and war.

For when they saw we were afraid,
how knowingly they played on every fear—
so conned, we scarcely saw their scorn,
hardly noticed as they took our funds, our rights,
and tapped our phones, turned back our clocks,
and then, to quell dissent, they sent . . .
(but here the document is torn)

THE GIRL WITH BEES IN HER HAIR

came in an envelope with no return address;
she was small, wore a wrinkled dress of figured
cotton, full from neck to ankles, with a button
of bone at the throat, a collar of torn lace.
She was standing before a monumental house
on the scale you see in certain English films:
urns, curved drives, stone lions, and an entrance far
too vast for any home. She was not of that place,
for she had a foreign look, and tangled black hair,
and an ikon, heavy and strange, dangling from
an oversized chain around her neck, that looked
as if some tall adult had taken it from his,
and hung it there as a charm to keep her safe
from a world of infinite harm that soon
would take him far from her, and leave her
standing, as she stood now—barefoot, gazing
without expression into distance, away
from the grandeur of that house, its gravel
walks and sculpted gardens. She carried a basket
full of flames, but whether fire, or flowers
with crimson petals shading toward a central gold,
was hard to say—though certainly, it burned,
and the light within it had nowhere else
to go, and so fed on itself, intensified its red
and burning glow, the only color in the scene.
The rest was done in grays, light and shadow
as they played along her dress, across her face,
and through her midnight hair, lively with bees.
At first they seemed just errant bits of shade,
until the humming grew too loud to be denied

as the bees flew in and out, as if choreographed
in a country dance between the fields of sun
and the black tangle of her hair.
                              Without warning
a window on one of the upper floors flew open—
wind had caught the casement, a silken length
of curtain filled like a billowing sail—the bees
began to stream out from her hair, straight
to the single opening in the high façade. Inside,
a moment later—the sound of screams.

The girl—who had through all of this seemed
unconcerned and blank—all at once looked up.
She shook her head, her mane of hair freed
of its burden of bees, and walked away,
out of the picture frame, far beyond
the confines of the envelope that brought her
image here—here, where the days grow longer
now, the air begins to warm, dread grows to
fear among us, and the bees swarm.

BE CAREFUL WHAT YOU REMEMBER

Can you see them now—the statues?
Can you see them, stirring on their pedestals,
trying out their stiff arms, stepping gingerly
down, breaking the glass walls that encase them?

At the Vatican, forcing the door of the locked
room, tearing off the plaster-of-paris fig leaves,
rummaging about in the heaps of broken-off
genitals, so that, when they leave God's palace of art,
like the eunuchs of China's final dynasty, who left
the palace for the last time, carrying in small jars
the parts of themselves taken by empire—
so too, the statues would be whole now, heading home.

They tear themselves from the fountains, leaving
behind the public play of the waters; climb down
from their candlelit niches, deserting
their place in the great composition. They enter
the long loneliness of roads, their exodus making
a path from the cities, a gleaming white stream
like refugees returning to their distant, burned villages,
their memories a desolation of marble.

Day and night they travel—some leading the horses
on which they've been mounted for years in piazzas,
their postures heroic. All were on foot, even
the gods, unaccustomed to walking; and angels
from tombstones—their wings hanging useless,
scholars and poets, tall women in togas, a boxer
with a broken nose, a hooded woman stumbling

under her son's dead weight, an armless Venus,
a headless Victory led by Justice—the blindfold
torn from her eyes. Their streams converging
on the road to the mountains, they climb higher
and higher, like salmon returning to the ponds
that had spawned them, the statues,
relentless, make their way to the quarries
from which they were hewn—
the opened veins
in the heart of the mountain.

An avalanche heard from a distance, rumbling
and thundering, or an earthquake, a war begun,
or a world ending—we could only guess
what we had heard. Then word spread that the statues
were missing: the fountains, the squares, the galleries
stood empty; the gardens were vacant,
the pedestals naked, the tombstones abstract.
And, it is true, where the quarries had been
(you can travel there and see for yourself)
the mountain is whole again, the great rift closed,
and young trees grow thick again on the slopes.

FROM
REVERSING THE SPELL,
NEW POEMS (1993–1996)

TRÜMMERFRAUEN
(THE RUBBLE-WOMEN)

I. △

In the old paintings, the ones with silken oils
whose vistas opened like a long hall to the eye,
the Virgin with her glowing skin, the child
in her arms, formed a perfect triangle—the art
historians always made a point of that: God
in Euclid's arms, the blue satin shawl and
temporary flesh fit in the pyramid of faith
exactly: abstract and equilateral; the baby held
in her painted lap, fattened for sacrifice;
while in the streets, blood ran, and skinny dogs
prowled the greasy cobblestones; monthly,
the women wore, then washed the red-stained
rags, and the candles in the church flickered
under the bloodless Lady with her lovely face,
under the nailed-up man, the body's long disgrace
impaled naked on the crossroads of the grid.

II. ▲

Outside the ruined church and the bombed
museum, the rubble piles stand along the road;
at the apex of each one, a woman sits, whatever
the weather, and with a little hammer breaks

the mortar from the broken stones. The women
atop the pyramids of rubble tap and tap, the sound
is like the ghostly tapping of woodpeckers in
the burned and blackened place the forest stood.

Behind each of these widow women on her heap
slowly rise the piles of finished stone. Here and there,
little fires still break out, a flurry of fiery ash, lines
of smoke unwinding the flat gray sky.

It is hard to tell the mortar from crushed bones:
a fine sift of gray wants to hang in the air
and to coat the hair of the women
who seem at times almost stone themselves

except for the sound of tapping and the way
the pile behind them grows, clean stone
ready for the mason, the architects
of a future that none of them can bear

to conceive—alone as they are, and cold.
But the relentless percussion of life goes on,
the little hammers rise and fall, descendants
of Thor, of Luther, whose hammers split

the Northern sky, the Christian world—
persistent, they tap and tap, the old mortar
flakes away like a fine snow of stone.
And what can be made of the altars now,

the broken walls of the fallen hearths,
when so much of the future has gone?
Elsewhere, no doubt, men are drawing up
their plans. Out here, the women sit,

each on her pile of stones, their hammers
never stop: *tap tap, tap tap, tap tap.*

MIDDLE-CLASS VANTAGE

We found this small, dry rise with a nice view,
the smell of pine, the sound of water running by,
and here we pitched our little canvas tent,

a temporary pyramid with an open side,
its flaps pulled back. The site is insignificant,
just a pleasant prospect and a place to rest:

the salmon run is past, the trout are small and
somnolent, the breeze is slight, the next town down
the road much like the one before—the general store,

the antique shop with its predictable little cups, chipped
pansy faces half worn off, the jewelry in a dusty case
from the sale of some estate, things lost without

their history, and maybe a Victorian house or two,
gaily painted in the palette of imaginary time, the color
of lilacs and ersatz lime, and here and there a real dog

to animate the scene. It's all a bit too green, quick water
in this drowsy channel slows, while autumn slides
its razor in the seams, the wind comes up,

the tent flaps stir, and something like a burr
sticks to the heart, and nothing can shake it off.
Situated as we are, we watch the river coursing on,

carrying whatever debris has fallen to its current ways,
and this is when we see familiar shapes go whirling by,
carried who knows where; helpless, we watch

from the banks, as we see ourselves float by—
all we can think to do is wave, wave from the water,
wave from the shore, hello, hello; goodbye, goodbye.

FACING INTO IT

So it is here, then, after so long, and after all—
as the light turns in the leaves in the old golden
way of fall,
          as the small beasts dig to the place
at the roots where survival waits, cowardly crouching
in the dark,
          as the branches begin to stretch into winter,
freed of their cheerful burden of green, then
        it comes home, the flea-ridden bitch of desolation,
a thin dog with its ribs exposed like a lesson
in mathematics, in subtraction; it comes home, to find its bowl
empty—then the numberless
things for which to be grateful dissolve
like the steam from a fire just doused with water
on a day of overcast grays, lined
by a cold slanting rain—
             it is October, that season when Death
goes public, costumed, when the talking heads
on the TV screen float up smiling at the terrible
news, their skin alight with the same strange glow
fish give off when they have been dead a week or more,
as the gas company adds odor for warning
that the lines may be leaking, the sweet smell of disaster
hanging, invisible, in the air, a moment
before you strike the match—

it is then, brother, that I think of you, of your Caravaggio,
of the head of Goliath swung by its hair,
wearing the artist's own weary expression,
exhausted of everything but its desire

for that beautiful David he used to be; and I think
of all the boys walking the streets
each carrying the severed head of the man
he will become—and the way I bear it is
to think of you, grinning, riding high in the cart leaving
the scene, a pair of huge horses hauling the wagon,
a fine mist rising from their damp shoulders,
unconcerned with what hangs, nailed
to the museum walls—luckily
the fall of Icarus has nothing to do with them,
nor the ruined Goliath who fell like a forest,
nor the wretched Salomes with their blood-splattered
platters, nor the huge stone griffins sobbing
at the gates to Valhalla as the litters are carried past . . .

the dark eyes of the horses are opaque with wisdom,
their hoofs strike the pavements with such a musical decision,
the derisive curl of their lips is so like the mysterious
smile on the angel at Chartres, on Kuan Yin, on the dolphin,
as they pull the cart safe through the blizzards
of Main St., the snow slowly swallowing the signs
though the crossing light beckons—
a soft glowing green like some spectral Eden
in the blank white swirl of the storm.
The stallion neighs once, sends a warm cloud
of breath into the snow-filled air,
and the mare isn't scared yet—at least
she's still pulling. There's a barn out there
somewhere, as they plow through the light's
yellow aura of caution, its warm glow
foretelling what hides in the storm:
a stall full of gold, where the soul—
that magician—can wallow
and winter in straw.

ON ETHNIC DEFINITIONS

In the Jewish Cemetery in Prague,
the ghetto was so small, so little
space for the living, and less (by rights)
for the dead—they were buried
standing up. Hear the underground
train to Sheol, packed
for the rush-hour of ghosts—when
the train arrives, when the final trump
sounds and the Saved dead rise,
with a sigh, they'll at last lie down.

OF A SUN SHE CAN REMEMBER

After they had been in the woods,
after the living tongue woke Helen's
hand, afterwards they went back
to the little house of exile, Annie and
Helen, who had lived in the silent
dark, like a bat without radar in
the back of a cave, and she picked up
the broken doll she had dismembered
that morning in her rage, and limb
by limb, her agile fingers moving
with their fine intelligence over each
part, she re-membered the little figure
of the human, and, though she
was inside now, and it was still dark,
she remembered the missing sun
with a slow wash of warmth
on her shoulders, on her back—
as when you step shivering out of
a dank shade into the sun's sudden
balm—and as the warmth spread,
it felt like the other side of water,
and that is when she knew how
light on water looks, and she put
her outspread hands into the idea
of it, and she lifted the lines of light,
cross-hatched like a web, out of
the water, and, dripping, stretched
the golden net of meaning in the light.

THE MESSENGER

The messenger runs, not carrying the news
    of victory, or defeat; the messenger, unresting,
has always been running, the wind before and behind him,
    across the turning back of earth, leaving
his tracks across the plains, his ropes
    hanging from the ledges of mountains;
for centuries, millennia, he has been running
    carrying whatever it is that cannot be
put down: it is rolled in a tube
    made of hide, carefully, to keep it dry
as he runs, through storms and monsoons,
    sometimes on foot, sometimes poling a boat
through a flooded mangrove swamp, or
    setting stiff sails to cross from island to island
running before the wind. In some ages, peasants
    have helped him—bringing him small cakes
of rice wrapped in the weeds of the sea and
    new sandals woven of hemp for his torn
bleeding feet; sometimes in the heat of noon
    they would offer a drink of rosewater, sometimes
a coat of fur against the winter snows;
    and sometimes at night, he would rest
by a fire where voices wove with the music
    of gut-strings, or with mountain pipes whose
sound was like wind through the bones
    of creation—and he would be cheered
by the company of others, the firelit glow
    of their faces like a bright raft afloat in the dark;
at times, rumors spread of his death, scholars
    analyzed his obsession, dated his bones, his prayer bundle;

but at dawn, he always arose, in the mists,
 in the blur of so many mornings, so many shoes
worn into scraps and discarded, so many
 the cities that burned as he passed
them, so many the skulls abandoned
 by armies, so many whose blood
stained the threads of their prayer rugs,
 so many, so many, so many—

 oh,
and that green, sunlit hill that kept
 rising from the dark waters of flood, outlined bright
against the sky, the odds, the evidence—
 and he, the messenger,
running through history, carries this small tube,
 its durable hide—carries it, not like
a torch, no, nothing so blazing;
 not like the brass lamp that summons
a genie, no magic wishes;
 not like the candles that hope sets aflame
and a breath can extinguish . . .

 no.
He carried it like
 what has no likeness,
what is curled up inside and
 he swore he could feel it, though
perhaps he had dreamed it, still
 at times, stopping under some tree
or other, when the night was warm,
so close the stars seemed to breathe in
the branches, he would lie quiet,
 then it would seem
that whatever it was in there
 would pulse softly with light, a code
only the heart could break

(but of course he couldn't say
for he was only the messenger)—

and at sunrise, wearily, he would rise
    to his feet and trudge on, sometimes
running, sometimes stumbling,
    carrying whatever it was that could not
be put down, would not be cast aside—
    and besides, he would chide himself,
weren't they all as tired as he,
    and hadn't they helped him, time
        and again, on his way?

UP AGAINST IT

The wall was white, whitewash lime
that shines in the sun till white is pure pain
searing the eyes.
                  And the wall was marked,
pocked by a spray of black holes, like nothing
so much as the dots in a child's puzzle, waiting
for a line to make sense of them, to pull
from a scatter of points, a familiar shape.

At the beginning of the bad time
we have come to think of as usual, they stood
a man here, against this wall, simply because
of what he was, something that made it hard
to do what they wanted,
                  so they thought that
if they killed him first, at the very beginning,
the rest would come easy, his blood like a red
door opening into the future in which the gypsy
wind, capricious, always eluding them,
would be stilled, tied in a sack;
and the everyday that wore them
down into grit under its heels would disappear
into clouds of power; their boots would be real
leather, the rawhide smell from what they had taken
and hadn't the time to cure.

And if he were Lorca, García Lorca, the writer
with a fire in his hands (and he was)—
and if they stood him up against this wall
in its white that defeated the light, throwing it back

like a knife into the eyes—and if, in that moment,
as they raised their guns, he remembered
a dream he had dreamed but a month
before, a dream of a lamb surrounded and butchered
by shepherds—

                  if all this were true (and it is)—then
we approach this wall at our cost, counting its black
holes like the shrunken emblems of the cosmos eating
back its own matter—and what then?

                      Shall we paste up the placards
of a revolution in which we no longer believe? Shall we
tear down the wall, knowing another stands behind it,
and another, and another, to the horizon of counting?
Shall we line up the children beside it,
pointing at each hole as a lesson
through which, like a sieve,
their hope will begin
to drain out?

Or shall we plant flowering vines along the wall
                to cover the record?
            And when each tendril, each slow,
    wavering filament,
                each unruly, winding line of green
   is swaying along the wall,
                  looking for somewhere to anchor
       its urge to go on growing
            (*verde, te quiero verde*),
                    what then?

Why, by then, in the long twilights, in the hard work
　　of planting and watering, of watching and waiting,
　　　　by then we may have understood what we can't now
　　　　　　imagine, desperate as we are about the white wall, the holes
　　　　　　　　in the shape of a man, the mark they wanted to leave us,
　　　　　　　　　　the line terror taught us to trace—
　　　　　　　　　　　　　　　　　　so different
　　　　　　　　　from the one that he left, the one whose
　　　　　　　　　　shape left its trace in the heart, the balcony open,
　　　　　　　　　　　the long spill of stars in the sky, the track
　　　　　　　　　　　　of creation's milky tongue, and, listen—
　　　　　　　　　　　the shift and seethe of the sap
　　　　　　　　　　　　　　forcing its slow way toward the branching
　　　　　　　　　　　　　　twigs—the ear-splitting crack
　　　　　　　　　　　　　　　　as the end is riven by budding—
　　　　　　　　　　　　　　　a salt breeze in the orchard,
　　　　　　　　　　　　　　　　　the small leaves trembling with light.

FROM
OTHERWISE (1993)

NIGHT FISHING IN THE SOUND

The sound is dark; you can barely hear
the gauze-wrapped warning song
of bells, and cannot see
the buoys swinging on top
the oily waves, the water a black
so absolute it drinks light
back, unquenchable thirst
like that the shades in Hades had
for the hot blood of sacrifice—
how the dead swell, like ticks,
till they rise, bloated envoys
out of the envious dark.

The waves of the sound sway
endlessly, a restless channel caught
between two seas—one fresh, the other salt—
as if suspended between hope and
certain sorrow. And you, in a small craft,
having left behind the little inland
sea, are tossed in all this roiling dark;
the trick is to play the wind
for time, sinking the line
deep into the heaving black, trying
not to stare at the dizzying lantern swinging
over the deck, a drunken sun on a pendulum;
trying to keep your equilibrium
with no horizon to steady the eye, riding
the dark sound blind, hoping for fish,
wanting to reel in, to reach the end
of the passage, but afraid

of the waiting ocean, the enormous dawn
when light, rising from below, seems to come
from everywhere at once, tsunami of
overwhelming sun.

But still there is
the solid feel of the helm
under your hand, worn grain
of wood that fits the grasp
and steers the little craft
out of the rocking cradle of the dark,
safe, into the cauldron of dawn.

BEING AS I WAS, HOW COULD I HELP . . .

It was the noise that drew me first,
even before the scent. The long water
had brought something to my den, spilling
its banks, leaving the hollow pod
of reeds in the cool mud. Whatever it was,
it cried inside, and an odor rose
from it—man-smell but sweeter.
Two small hairless cubs were in it, pink
as summer oleander, waving
the little worm-like things they had
instead of paws. Naked like that, they
made my blood go slow, my dugs
begin to drip. I tipped the pod, they slid
into the ferns, I nuzzled the howling
pair, they found my side, they suckled
there and drank their fill. That night
the red star in the sky was bright,
a vulture's eye that waits
with a patience that I hardly understand.
The twin cubs slept in their shining
skin, warm at my side. I dreamed:

The trees were falling, one by one,
the sound deafening, the dust that rose
from one a mist to hide the felling
of the next. The mountains were
cut in two; great stones were rolled
and piled like hills until the sky
was shut; where the trees
had grown, pillars of stone rose

high, the birds circled, but
their skulls struck the sky.
Teeth chewed the earth; our den fell in
like a rotted log when weight is
added to decay; nothing to eat, the cubs
howled, the flesh fell from our bones,
we ran under a strange sky whose light
was wrong: it rose from the city walls,
bounced off the leaden heaven—flat
as the sound of a stone striking mud.
One of the brothers killed the other.
Blood poured where the streams had run.

Nowhere to drink, we slink from one rock
to the next, hunger drives us to the walls
where, sharp as the eyes of men, death
waits with its thousand iron thorns.

But the warm sun woke me. I forgot.
The twins were all I saw, for days
we lay together by the den, the river
ran beside us like a friend; they drank
and laughed at the morning light
that played in the shelter
of the leaves. Forgive me,
I was wolf, and could not help
the love that flowed from me to them,
the thin sweet river of milk.
Even now, though the world has come
to match the dream, I think
I would give it again.

THE MUSE

There she was, for centuries, the big
broad with the luscious tits, the secret
smile, a toga of translucent silk, cool
hand on the shoulder of the suffering
poet—the tease who made him
squeeze those great words out. He
was the mirror and the lamp, she the torch
who burned with the blue butane of a pure
refusal, too good for mortal use, her breath
was cold as mountain streams, the chill
of the eternal—no hint of plaque
or any odor of decay. Ethereal as hell,
a spirit in chiffon, the mystery is
how she had got so rounded in the butt
and all her better parts as soft as butter,
why such a wraith should be so ample,
what her endowments had to do
with that for which she set example—
all this was surely Mystery, oh that elusive
object of desire, that *unravish'd bride
of quietness*, that plump poetic dish
who lived on air but looked
as if she dined on pasta.

Basta! A pox on the great Lacan
who writes with his eraser, on all poetic
Graces, mute and pensive, concave exactly
where he is most extensive—oh look
what she has *not* that he has got,
a thing I'm too polite to mention
except to say it rhymes with Venus,
it was the Latin word for tail;
its root, therefore, is *not* the same as pen
which comes from the word for feather.

But enough of these fine distinctions.
What a great tradition was born when
Alexander whipped his penknife out, cut
the knot she carefully had tied, leaped
on his mount, a perfect straddle,
and let the crotch decide
who was the horse and who was the rider,
who was the muse and who
the writer.

THE BIRD IN THE LAUREL'S SONG

"How long have I been here? I can't recall
how many suns have risen and withdrawn
since I came down to this branch to rest.

How strange it felt at first, warm
under my feet, and when I landed here
and clamped my claws around its bark
I could have sworn I heard a moan. Is this
the work of men, I wondered then,
who like to decoy us with images of wood
we take for friend, then lay in wait for us, armed,
their arrows tipped with our own feathers.
Yet this was opposite of that—a tree that feels
like wood, an ordinary laurel, leaves a polished
green, but with a pulse inside, I swear,
the engine of a heart like mine; and something
not quite planted in its stance—the way it swayed
and seemed to reach out toward me as I passed.
And so I stopped, and sat.
                              But I'm uneasy
now, the forest ways are broken here,
some sadness haunts this tree
that I fear, mortally, to sound. Nor can I sing
when these leaves rustle in the air
around my perch, and breathe and whisper
in my ear, and speak of what I cannot
bear, nor compass with my airborne
mind—some deep attachment to the ground
whose price is to be rooted there; it makes
my wings ache with the thought, and

I must fly away from here—but yet am held
in dappled light like a net of lace
that will not let me go. O gods,
if you can break the spell that holds us
both together in this glade, then I will
stay with what it is within that suffers here."

      The laurel stirred in a passing wind, and the sun,
      liquid light on the river's back, moved
      in a shiver of gold, and a woman appeared
      by the river's bank, looked around
      as if awakened from a dream, a little dazed.
      She reached down to pick the book up
      that had fallen at her side, and following
      the river's edge, she wandered off,
      singing to herself.

      "But it was I who sang,
though I look out through her eyes;
it is I whom the gods hear, I who laid down
my wings, and nested here out of love."

UME: PLUM

The fruit is small, and often served
shriveled, soaked in some attar or
other, an odd shade of red, weak and
toward the blue. Sometimes one
of these unpromising tiny plums
is set in the center
of a flat bed of white rice, to mime
the nation's flag—red sun
on a white field. Those years ago, we never
knew, kept ignorant of all that might
disable war, that the flag with the wide
red rays, that rose over the bodies,
adorned the Zero's wings, was a war flag,
emblem of a burning sun, like rage
or whatever it is that sets men's lives
at nought, and pours them, young
and hot, down history's drain.

The trees here must be bred for the beauty
of their flower, for the plums are sour, the cherries
small and bitter—but, oh, the *ume* blooming
in the early spring, the *sakura* unfolding
in a brilliant sky, blossoms borrowing
the light for shelter—a glowing parasol
of pink and white, or
the world a child's globe
that sits in the Buddha's hand
and when he laughs, it shakes, until
the air is filled with silken snow,
the wind toying with it, lifting

the petals as if back to the branch,
then bringing them lightly down.

Walking the shimmering tunnel of flowering
trees along the Imperial moat, Mrs. Nakano
and I spoke of the war, when we were
both children (the same age, I think,
though it was a point of pride with her
to never say). Her voice was
matter of fact, or else it was
the way English goes flat in a mouth
made for another tongue.
In Kobe, she had crouched with her
mother in the bomb shelter while our
planes bombed her city flat. The trees
shivered a little, the delicate arbor
sent down a shower of petals
to our feet. The carp, grown huge, slid by
in the moat, and the rain began, steady;
we opened our umbrellas
as we went. She spoke then
about her husband, her misery
with him, his anger, and his mother,
the doors that one by one
she'd tried and found them locked.

How do we keep from going mad? I thought, looking
at the trees bred for their beauty
by an aesthetic breed of men, who
wanted a woman wrapped in tissue-thin silk,
her mouth a hole with blackened teeth,
who would dive at the dark stack of a ship
to a fiery death. And saw, with them, our own
young men, the same, filing into the black
belly of a huge cargo plane, each with a woman
in his wallet, her words on lilac paper,

her distant image as his aphrodisiac
in hell. I tried to ask the question that can't
be asked in words—having no subject and no predicate
but death. I thought of the bombs falling, and
then my mind went blank as the radar screen
when the thing that moves into its range
is much too close, or gone.

And Mrs. Nakano and I, the fortunate ones,
walked side by side beneath the cherry trees
and watched the great smoking craters
of memory fill in and disappear, and watched
the rain turn the fallen petals
into a sticky debris, and walked
because we were alive, and walked
to keep from going mad, and walked
for beauty, and for company,
the whole perimeter of the Emperor's moat,
that carp-infested fence around
the palace, walled in,
where power keeps its face,
and ends, as history ends, in Lear—
old, heartsore—the dead
Cordelia in his arms. Reverse pietà,
a motherless world, the father
holding the sacrificed child
on a ground of fallen petals
wet with rain, plum
on a field of white.

But here, we break the circle, cross
the street, and bow.
We part, Mrs. Nakano
and I, go, each
to her own
gate.

BAT CAVE

The cave looked much like any other
from a little distance but
as we approached, came almost
to its mouth, we saw its walls within
that slanted up into a dome
were beating like a wild black lung—
it was plastered and hung with
the pulsing bodies of bats, the organ
music of the body's deep
interior, alive, the sacred cave
with its ten thousand gleaming eyes
near the clustered rocks
where the sea beat with the leather
wings of its own dark waves.

Below the bat-hung, throbbing walls,
an altar stood, glittering with guano,
a stucco sculpture like a Gaudí
church, berserk
Baroque, stone translated into
flux—murk and mud and the floral
extravagance of wet sand dripped
from a giant hand, giving back
blessing, excrement—return
for the first fruits offered to the gods.

We stayed outside, superior
with fear, like tourists
peering through a door, whose hanging
beads rattle in the air from

one who disappeared into the dim
interior; we thought of the caves
of Marabar, of a man who entered
and never quite emerged—
the caves' echoing black
emptiness a tunnel in the English
soul where he is wandering still. So
the bat cave on the Bali coast, not far
from Denpasar, holds us off, and beckons . . .

Standing there now, at the mouth
of the cave—this time we enter, feel
inside the flutter of those
many hearts, the radiant heat of pumping
veins, the stretch of wing on bone
like a benediction, and the familiar
faces of this many-headed god,
benevolent as night is
to the weary—the way at dark
the cave releases them all,
how they must lift like the foam
on a wave breaking, how many
they are as they enter
the starlit air, and scatter
in wild wide arcs
in search of fruit, the sweet bites
of mosquito . . .

while the great domes of our
own kind slide open, the eye
that watches, tracks the skies,
and the huge doors roll slowly back
on the hangars, the planes
push out their noses of steel,
their wings a bright alloy

of aluminum and death, they roar
down the runways, tear into
the night, their heavy bodies fueled
from sucking at the hidden
veins of earth; they leave a trail of fire
behind them as they scar
the air, filling the dreams
of children, sleeping—anywhere,
Chicago, Baghdad—with blood,
as the bombs drop, as the world
splits open, as the mothers
reach for their own
in the night of the falling
sky, madness in
method, nature gone
into reverse . . .

here, nearly unperturbed,
the bats from the sacred cave
fill the night with their calls,
high-pitched, tuned to the solid world
as eyes to the spectrum of light, gnats
to the glow of a lamp—the bats
circle, the clouds wheel,
the earth turns
pulling the dome of stars
among the spinning trees, blurring
the sweet globes of fruit, shaped
exactly to desire—dizzy, we swing
back to the cave on our stiff dark
wings, the sweet juice of papaya
drying on our jaws, home
to the cave, to attach ourselves
back to the pulsing dome, until,
hanging there, sated and sleepy,

we can see what was once our world
upside down as it is
and wonder whose altars
those are, white,
encrusted with shit.

RHAPSODY, WITH RAIN

In Hawai'i the rain comes down hard,
friendly, the forest is used to it,
the flowers in their profusion
a perennial thirst. A woman stands
in the open doorway of her house,
dreaming of Maine, of thunder and
the leaves of the maple turning
to face familiar weather. But the child
has never known anything but
the rains of Hawai'i, its trees
laden with blossoms, the stars
in the night sky so much like
the small white sweet flowers
in the dark green hedge by the door
that the heavens too must be
perfumed to the very edge
of infinitude—he doesn't yet
think these things but he is filled
with them, all the same. He stands,
leaning toward the falling water,
holding his mother's leg
for support, this little
Noah, untroubled
by the freight his name carries,
small steward of the future,
loving these rains, seeing
only the shining veils
of his bridal with
the world, standing
on the rim of the Pacific

on his island that is all of earth
to him, boundless, secure,
standing on the threshold of
the house of Sarah and Matthew,
greeting the rain.

FROM
SARAH'S CHOICE (1989)

READING THE BIBLE BACKWARDS

All around the altar, huge lianas
curled, unfurled the dark green
of their leaves to complement the red
of blood spilled there—a kind of Christmas
decoration, overhung with heavy vines
and over them, the stars.
When the angels came, messengers like birds
but with the oiled flesh of men, they hung
over the scene with smoldering swords,
splashing the world when they beat
their rain-soaked wings against the turning sky.

The child was bright in his basket
as a lemon, with a bitter smell from his wet
swaddling clothes. His mother bent
above him, singing a lullaby
in the liquid tongue invented
for the very young—short syllables
like dripping from an eave
mixed with the first big drops of rain
like tiny silver pears, from
the glistening fronds of palm. The three
who gathered there—old kings uncrowned:
the cockroach, condor, and the leopard, lords
of the cracks below the ground, the mountain
pass and the grass-grown plain—were not
adorned, did not bear gifts, had not
come to adore; they were simply drawn
to gawk at this recurrent, awkward son
who the wind had said would spell

the end of earth as it had been.
Somewhere north of this familiar scene
the polar caps were melting, the water was
advancing in its slow, relentless
lines, swallowing the old
landmarks, swelling the
seas that pulled
the flowers and the great steel cities down.
The dolphins sport in the rising sea,
anemones wave their many arms like hair
on a drowned gorgon's head, her features
softened by the sea beyond all recognition.

On the desert's edge where the oasis dies
in a wash of sand, the sphinx seems to shift
on her haunches of stone, and the rain, as it runs down,
completes the ruin of her face. The Nile
merges with the sea, the waters rise
and drown the noise of the earth. At the forest's
edge, where the child sleeps, the waters gather—
as if a hand were reaching for the curtain
to drop across the glowing, lit tableau.

When the waves closed over, completing the green
sweep of ocean, there was no time for mourning.
No final trump, no thunder to announce
the silent steal of waters; how soundlessly
it all went under: the little family
and the scene so easily mistaken
for an adoration. Above, more clouds poured in
and closed their ranks against the skies;
the angels, who had seemed so solid, turned
quicksilver in the rain.
                              Now, nothing but the wind
moves on the rain-pocked face
of the swollen waters, though far below

where giant squid lie hidden in shy tangles,
the whales, heavy-bodied as the angels,
their fins like vestiges of wings,
sing some mighty epic of their own—

a great day when the ships would all withdraw,
the harpoons fail of their aim, the land
dissolve into the waters, and they would swim
among the peaks of mountains, like eagles
of the deep, while far below them, the old
nightmares of earth would settle
into silt among the broken cities, the empty
basket of the child would float
abandoned in the seaweed until the work of water
unraveled it in filaments of straw,
till even that straw rotted
in the planetary thaw the whales prayed for,
sending their jets of water skyward
in the clear conviction they'd spill back
to ocean with their will accomplished
in the miracle of rain: *And the earth*
was without form and void, and darkness
was upon the face of the deep. And
the Spirit moved upon the face of the waters.

SARAH'S CHOICE

A little late rain   *The testing*
the desert in the beauty of its winter   *of Sarah*
bloom, the cactus ablaze
with yellow flowers that glow
even at night in the reflected light
of moon and the shattered crystal of sand
when time was so new
that God still walked
among the tents, leaving no prints
in the sand, but a brand burned into
the heart—on such a night
it must have been, although
it is not written in the Book
how God spoke to Sarah
what he demanded of her
how many questions came of it
how a certain faith was
fractured, as a stone is split
by its own fault, a climate of extremes
and one last drastic change
in the temperature.

"Go!" said the Voice. "Take your son,
your only son, whom you love,
take him to the mountain, bind him
and make of him a burnt offering."
Now Isaac was the son of Sarah's age,
a gift, so she thought, from God. And how
could he ask her even to imagine such a thing—

to take the knife
of the butcher and thrust it
into such a trusting heart, then
light the pyre on which tomorrow burns.
What fear could be more holy
than the fear of *that*?

"Go!" said the Voice, Authority's own.
And Sarah rose to her feet, stepped out
of the tent of Abraham to stand between
the desert and the distant sky, holding its stars
like tears it was too cold to shed.
Perhaps she was afraid the firmament
would shudder and give way, crushing her
like a line of ants who, watching
the ants ahead marching safe under the arch,
are suddenly smashed by the heel
they never suspected. For Sarah,
with her desert-dwelling mind, could
see the grander scale in which the heel
might simply be the underside of some Divine
intention. On such a scale, what is
a human son? So there she stood, absurd
in the cosmic scene, an old woman bent
as a question mark, a mote in the eye
of God. And then it was that Sarah spoke
in a soft voice, a speech
the canon does not record.

"No," said Sarah to the Voice.   *The*
"I will not be chosen. Nor shall my son—   *teachings*
if I can help it. You have promised Abraham,   *of Sarah*
through this boy, a great nation. So either
this sacrifice is sham, or else it is a sin.
Shame," she said, for such is the presumption

of mothers, "for thinking me a fool,
for asking such a thing. You must have known
I would choose Isaac. What use have I
for History—an arrow already bent
when it is fired from the bow?"

Saying that, Sarah went into the tent
and found her restless son awake, as if he had
grown aware of the narrow bed in which he lay.
And Sarah spoke out of the silence
she had herself created, or that had been there
all along. "Tomorrow you will be
a man. Tonight, then, I must tell you
the little that I know. You can be chosen
or you can choose. Not both.

The voice of the prophet grows shrill.
He will read even defeat as a sign
of distinction, until pain itself
becomes holy. In that day, how shall we tell
the victims from the saints,
the torturers from the agents of God?"
"But mother," said Isaac, "if we were not God's
chosen people, what then should we be? I am afraid
of being nothing." And Sarah laughed.

Then she reached out her hand. "Isaac,   *The*
I am going now, before Abraham awakes, before   *unbinding*
the sun, to find Hagar the Egyptian and her son   *of Isaac*
whom I cast out, drunk as I was on pride,
God's promises, the seed of Abraham
in my own late-blooming loins."

"But Ishmael," said Isaac, "how should I greet him?"
"As you greet yourself," she said, "when you bend

over the well to draw water and see your image,
not knowing it reversed. You must know your brother
now, or you will see your own face looking back
the day you're at each other's throats."

She wrapped herself in a thick dark cloak
against the desert's enmity, and tying up
her stylus, bowl, some dates, a gourd
for water—she swung her bundle on her back,
reached out once more toward Isaac.

"It's time," she said. "Choose now."

"But what will happen if we go?" the boy
Isaac asked. "I don't know," Sarah said.

"But it is written   what will happen   if you stay."

THE LAST MAN

Here, in our familiar streets, the day
is brisk with winter's business,
the reassuring rows of brick façades,
litter baskets overflowing
with the harvest of the streets,
and, when the light turns, the people
move in unison, the cars miraculously
slide to a stop, no one is killed,
the streets, for some reason, do not
show the blood that is pouring
like a tide, on other shores.

    Martinez, the last farmer left alive
    in his village, refuses to run, hopes
    that God, *El Salvador*,
    will let him get the harvest in.
    "Can a fish live out of water?" he says
    for why he stays, and weeds
    another row, ignoring the fins
    of sharks that push up
    through the furrows.

Here, it is said, we live
in the belly of the beast. Ahab sits
forever at the helm, his skin
white wax, an effigy. The whale carries
him, lashed to its side by the rope
from his own harpoon. His eyes
are dead. His ivory leg

juts from the flank of Leviathan
like a useless tooth.

> One more time, the little sail appears,
> a cloud forms, an old ikon for mercy
> turned up in a dusty corner
> of the sky, preparing rain
> for the parched land, Rachel
> weeping for her children. "Can a fish
> live out of water?" he asks again,
> and the rain answers in Spanish,
> *manitas de plata*
> little hands of silver on his brow.

MIRIAM'S SONG

Death to the first-born sons, always—
the first fruits to the gods of men.
She had not meant it so, standing in the reeds
back then, the current tugging at her skirt
like hands, she had only meant to save
her little brother, Moses,
red-faced with rage when he was given
to the river. The long curve of the Nile
would keep their line, the promised land
around the bend. Years later
when the gray angel, like the smoke trail
of a dying comet, passed by the houses
with blood smeared over doorways,
Miriam, her head hot in her hands, wept
as the city swelled with the wail of Egypt's women.
Then she straightened up, slowly plaited
her hair and wound it tight around her head,
drew her long white cloak with its deep blue threads
around her, went out to watch the river
where Osiris in his golden funeral barge
floated by forever . . .

as if in offering, she placed a basket on the river,
this time an empty one, without the precious cargo
of tomorrow. She watched it drift a little
from the shore. She threw one small stone in it,
then another, and another, till its weight
was too much for the water and it slowly turned
and sank. She watched the Nile gape and shudder,
then heal its own green skin. She went

to join the others, to leave one ruler
for another, one Egypt for the next.

Some nights you can still see her, by some river
where the willows hang, listening to the heavy tread
of armies, those sons once hidden dark
in baskets, and in her mind she sees her sister,
the black-eyed Pharaoh's daughter, lift the baby
like a gift from the brown floodwaters
and take him home to save him, such a pretty
boy and so disarming, as his dimpled hands
reach up, his mouth already open
for the breast.

POSTSCRIPT

to Maxine Kumin

Dear Max. I call you that because
two syllables are too much for the sharp
pain your poems cause, the ache
between the shoulder blades, from
what the older centuries called
heart. You're right
and there is something you can do, I can't:
say "I" and "love" and "gone" and
cut it right, neat as a split cord of wood,
the exact heft of the axe,
the straight, swift stroke.

Last week I tried to saw
a dead branch off the firethorn, and halfway
through I had to stop, not knowing
what I'd do when the damn thing started
falling . . . standing there, imagining
how it would pull down the power lines,
the wires for the phone, the healthy branch
below, and then, as it tore down
through all the wreckage of those lines
and ruined garden, it would hit me,
its thorns tear through my scalp,
put out my eyes and leave me bleeding
for the neighbors to discover. This sad
and total inability to cut
a simple branch down from the tree
when it was dead a year, this image
like some cheap disaster

film, makes me afraid
of scissors and of saw, of lighting fires,
of using "I," for fear I'll start
some mad striptease of art, tell all,
embarrass everyone, even the dog,

and bring the gossip-hounds to sniff
the ruins, the mess I made of it all,
like some baroque explosion in a clean
well-lighted room, and then climb out
onto the windowsill and hoot and
hoot like some demented owl, her feathers
damp from her own rain of tears,
trying to reel back the years, and not the ones
behind, that any fool
would not repeat, but those ahead
that speed up like a train
whose rails I'm tied to
like some poor, abandoned heroine
in a film that everyone is in
so no one wants to see it
over. And yet when you, refusing
both amnesia and the comfort of a myth,
can talk as straight as one might
hold a saw to get the dead branch down,
somehow, you save the tree.

While I can't face
the amputation of a branch without
the towers of Troy beginning to go over
like Humpty Dumpty toppling through the years,
his scattered bits the Hittites, the Sumerians,
the French in the deep freeze of the Russian
snow, and don't forget the Jews, the Congolese,
the British Empire shrinking to
tin soldiers on the counterpane,

and next America and all that now lives
with her, and then the planet like
a candle sputters out, and the sun
begins to fail in the heavens
and the cold sky fills
with an avalanche of angels, overweight,
falling though their feathers, with
burning hair like figures out of Blake,
and the planets break
their orbits and collide, the firmament
begins to crack and those old waters
that the Fathers said lay just beyond it
pour through the cracks in torrents,
close over everything (except this sonorous
voice-over, this announcer, who seems
to live out universal floods
and still not skip a beat, or miss
a comma)—

        you see, I find myself
in a false position and wish
some sanity would overtake me, like
Don Quijote unhorsed by the Knight
of Mirrors, and just say: dear,
could you just manage
to pull yourself together, take out
the trash and understand the universal
crash is not your business; your flight
from simply stating, from talking straight
as Max, is not being able
to do what Albrecht Dürer did
in just one simple drawing
in his notebook, shortly
before his own untimely death (for
whose death is not untimely?).
It was a portrait of himself, a naked man,

his right arm bent and pointing
at his middle, and written there
below it, just one line,
no easier in German:
"Here, it hurts."

CLASSICAL PROPORTIONS OF THE HEART

Everyone here knows how it ends,
in the stone amphitheater of the world, everyone
knows the story—how Jocasta
in her chamber hung herself for shame
how Oedipus tore out his eyes and stalked
his darkened halls crying
aaiiee aaiiee woe woe is me woe

These things everyone expects, shifting
on the cold stone seats, the discomfort
of our small, hard place in things
relieved by this public show of agony
how we love this last bit best, the wait
always worth it: the mask with its empty
eyes, the sweet sticky horror of it all
the luxurious wailing, the release;
the polis almost licking its lips
craning our necks to make out the wreck—
the tyrant brought low, howling
needing at last to lean
on a mere daughter, Antigone, who
in the sequel will inherit
her father's flair for the dramatic
her mother's acquaintance with death;
her hatred of falsehood, her own.

We feel a little superior, our seats
raised above the circle where the blinded
lion paces out his grief, selfcondemned
who could not keep his mastery to the end

(so Creon taunts him). What a flush
of pleasure stains our faces then
at the slow humiliation of an uncommon man
a Classical Golgotha without God, only
an eyeless wisdom, Apollo useless
against age, guilt, bad temper
and, most of all, against Laius
whose fear twisted the oracle's tongue,
childhater, the father who started it all.

The same night, as the howls rose
from the palace of Oedipus, the crowd
rising, drawing on their cloaks to go home,
far from the stage, that dramatic circle
that fixed our gaze, out there
on the stony hills gone silver under the moon
in the dry Greek air, the shepherd sits
he who saved the baby from the death
plotted by Laius, he who disobeyed a king
for pity's sake. Sitting there alone
under the appalling light of the stars
what does he think of how the gods
have used him, used his kind heart
to bait the trap of tragedy?
What brief can he make for mercy
in a world that Laius rules?

Sitting there, the moon his only audience,
perhaps he weeps, perhaps he feels
the planetary chill alone out there
on what had been familiar hills.
Perhaps he senses still the presence
of the Sphinx. And maybe
that is when he feels the damp
nudge against his hand.
By reflex, we could guess, he reaches out

to touch the coat of wool, begins
to stroke the lamb. "It's late," he says
at last, and lifts the small beast
to his chest, carrying it down
the treacherous stony path toward home, holding
its warmth against him. There is little drama
in this scene, but still its pathos has
a symmetry, because the lamb's small heat
up close exactly balances
the distant icy stars,
and when it senses home, and bleats,
its small cry weighs against
the wail of fallen kings.
There is, as well, the perfect closure
as the shepherd's gate swings shut
and a classical composure
in the way he bears
the burden of his heavy heart
with ease.

CONVERSATION WITH A JAPANESE STUDENT

That lovely climbing vine, so fresh
at dawn, so shy at noon, whose blue
countenance we call Morning Glory, you
call it *asakao*, Morning Face.
"What is this glory," you ask, child
of *akarui*, even the memory of war
effaced. "What is it all *for*?"

Here is an artist working, his brush
is history's tongue, his canvas
allegorical and large, the landscape
must be ample for his theme—
the turn of epic tides, pulled
in the wake of a dream. Glory,
unlike her homely twin, Mortality,
casts no shadow, never rests
("A beautiful and charming Female
Floating Westward through the air,
bearing on her forehead
the Star of Empire"). There,

notice that Glory is artfully draped
in a tunic of pale silk in the Classical style
her limbs as plump and supple
as oil paint and appetite
can make them, the lift of her head—proud,
a summons and a dare, one delicious arm
carries a bright banner streaming in the air
its design illegibly wrought

with large suggestions. But of Glory
you can be sure because
an army marches in her train—
almost a shadow, darkening the land.
At times, a peasant woman
raising her gaunt baby in a trite appeal
may momentarily block the light, obscure
Glory, put a little in the shade
all that golden beauty
the toss of whose curls is worth
a thousand ships, a million
villages, the world

for even a glimpse, the faintest rustle
of the hem of Beatrice's skirt
as it disappears around the corner
of those gates of pearl to the eternal
harbor, the flutter of doves
in the white thighs of Helen, desire
in its perfected form. The mirror of art
becomes a burning glass in the light
of absolute desire, the brush a flame
about to be consumed, for he has reached
the limits, here, of art—as Michelangelo
one night when he was old, in his rage
at the stubborn stone's refusal
to yield to his conception, attacked
his last Pietà with his chisel
trying to tear the pattern from the matter,
Christ from the arms of his grieving
mother; his servant
was forced to subdue the master
in order to save the work.

This time, no servant soul to intervene
and fire at the core, the center

split—as if mankind, with its cold
forever mind, trapped in its furious, failing heart,
had torn the Pietà apart from within—gone
the mother, a cloud of glowing dust,
gone the son, dissolved
in the monstrous cloud, heaven's fungus
growing on the axis of the world
casting its white shadow on the hills
pitiless as any parasite
whose life depends
on what it slowly kills.

No brush can paint a light so pure
          only the blind can see   white hot
      it whites out everything   but what is not
the sun's high noon, but brighter . . .

"*ex occidente, lex; ex Oriente, lux*"
          out of the West, law; out of the East, light.

At Nagasaki in the Peace Park near
the epicenter of the blast
there is a glade
so dense with foliage, bushes, *asakao*
and pine, you'd almost miss the sign, hand-drawn,
the only one in English that I saw:

THEY SAID NOTHING WOULD GROW HERE
    FOR 75 YEARS

And though the language was my own
I found it difficult to read
through such a thick exquisite screen
of evergreen
and tears.

HIGH NOON AT LOS ALAMOS

To turn a stone
with its white squirming
underneath, to pry the disc
from the sun's eclipse—white heat
coiling in the blinded eye: to these malign
necessities we come
from the dim time of dinosaurs
who crawled like breathing lava
from the earth's cracked crust, and swung
their tiny heads above the lumbering tons
of flesh, brains no bigger than a fist
clenched to resist the white flash
in the sky the day the sun-flares
pared them down to relics for museums,
turned glaciers back, seared Sinai's
meadows black—the ferns withered, the swamps
were melted to molten mud, the cells
uncoupled, recombined, and madly
multiplied, huge trees toppled to the ground,
the slow life there abandoned hope,
a caterpillar stiffened in the grass.
Two apes, caught in the act of coupling,
made a mutant child
who woke to sunlight wondering, his mother
torn by the huge new head
that forced the narrow birth canal.

As if compelled to repetition
and to unearth again
white fire at the heart of the matter—fire

we sought and fire we spoke,
our thoughts, however elegant, were fire
from first to last—like sentries set to watch
at Argos for the signal fire
passed peak to peak from Troy
to Nagasaki, triumphant echo of the burning
city walls and prologue to the murders
yet to come—we scan the sky
for that bright flash,
our eyes white from watching
for the signal fire that ends
the epic—a cursed line
with its caesura, a pause
to signal peace, or a rehearsal
for the silence.

FROM
SHEKHINAH (1984)

EMIGRATION

There are always, in each of us,
these two: the one who stays,
the one who goes away—
Charlotte, who stayed in the rectory
and helped her sisters die in England;
Mary Taylor, who went off to Australia
and set up shop with a woman friend.
"Charlotte," Mary said to her, "you are all
like potatoes growing in the dark."
And Charlotte got a plaque in Westminster
Abbey; Mary we get a glimpse of
for a moment, waving her kerchief
on the packet boat, and disappearing.
No pseudonym for her, and nothing
left behind, no trace
but a wide wake closing.

Charlotte stayed, and paid and paid—
the little governess with the ungovernable
heart, that she put on the altar.
She paid the long indemnity of all
who work for what will never wish them well,
who never set a limit to what's owed
and cannot risk foreclosure. So London
gave her fame, though it could never
sit comfortably with her at dinner—
how intensity palls when it is
plain and small and has no fortune.
When she died with her unborn child
the stars turned east

to shine in the gum trees of Australia,
watching over what has sidetracked evolution,
where Mary Taylor lived,
to a great old age, Charlotte's letters in a box
beside her bed, to keep her anger hot.

God bless us everyone until we sicken,
until the soul is like a little child
stricken in its corner by the wall; so there is
one who always sits there under lamplight
writing, staying on, and one
who walks the strange hills of Australia,
far too defiant of convention for the novels
drawn daily from the pen's "if only"—
if only Emily had lived,
if only they'd had money, if only
there had been a man who'd loved them truly
when all the time there had been
Mary Taylor, whom no one would remember
except she had a famous friend named Charlotte
with whom she was so loving-angry,
who up and left to be a woman
in that godforsaken outpost past
the reach of fantasy, or fiction.

WITHOUT REGRET

Nights, by the light of whatever would burn:
tallow, tinder and the silken rope
of wick that burns slow, slow
we wove the baskets from the long gold strands
of wheat that were another silk: worm soul
spun the one, yellow seed in the dark soil, the other.

The fields lay fallow, swollen with frost,
expectant winter. Mud clung to the edges
of our gowns; we had hung back like shadows
on the walls of trees and watched. In the little circles
that our tapers threw, murdered men rose red
in their clanging armor, muttered
words that bled through the bars
of iron masks: *the lord*
who sold us to the glory fields, lied.

Trumpets without tongues, we wove lilies
into the baskets. When they asked us
what we meant by these, we'd say "mary, mary"
and be still. We lined the baskets on the sill
in the barn, where it is always dusk
and the cows smell sweet. Now the snow

sifts through the trees, dismembered
lace, the white dust of angels, angels.
And the ringing of keys that hang
in bunches at our waists, and the sound of silk
whispering, whispering.
There is nothing in the high windows

but swirling snow,
the glittering milk of winter.
The halls grow chill. The candles flicker.
Let them wait who will and think what they want.
The lord has gone with the hunt, and the snow,
the snow grows thicker. Well he will keep
till spring thaw comes. Head, hand, and heart—
baskets of wicker, baskets of straw.

ARS POETICA

They wanted from us
loud despairs, ear-
splitting syntactical tricks, our guts
hung up to the light, privacy
dusted off and displayed, in ways
elliptical and clever, or
in a froth of spleen—details
of the damages, musings on divorce,
ashtrays from motels: films shot
on location, life made almost real
by its private dislocations. This,
they said, was the true
grit, the way it is, no lies, the heart
laid open as a pancake griddle to the awful
heat of rage, rage and desire, coiled beneath
and glowing, until even a drop of sweat
or ink, let fall in its vicinity,
would sizzle. And over it all, the big I
swollen like a jellyfish, quivering
and venomous. These things were
our imperative: the poet
in his stained t-shirt, all gripes
and belly, and, well, so *personable*—
my god, so like ourselves!
Oh yes, the women poets too, so
unashamed, ripping off their masks
like nylon stockings.

And all the time, the shy and shapely
mind, like some Eurydice, wanders—
darkened by veils, a shade
with measured footsteps. So many things are gone
and the end of the world looms
like a shark's fin on the flats of our horizon.
Fatigue sets in, and the wind rises.
The door is swinging on its hinges—the room
pried open, the one upstairs in Bluebeard's castle.
They have been hanging there a long time
in their bridal dresses, from hooks,
by their own long hair.
The wind that makes them sway until
they seem almost alive
is like the rush of our compassion.
Yes, now we remember them all
and the sea with its unchanging heaving—a grief
as deep and as dactylic as the voice of Homer,
and, as we turn another way, we lay the past out
on Achilles' shield, abandon it to earth,
our common ground—the bridal hope, its murder,
the old, old story, perpetual
as caring: the scant human store
that is so strangely self-restoring
and whose sufficiency
is our continual surprise.

THE WORLD IS NOT A MEDITATION

Odysseus, Penelope
that aging wife with a fixed idea—Odysseus.
Strange pair to put against the blare of sirens
on the news, prime-time wars that flicker
through the brain—still through it all:
one man lashed to a mast, one woman
tied by her own hair to a loom.

She nods a little at her work, her hands
fall idle in her lap. By now, she isn't sure
what she is waiting for; her mind
wanders,
she has stopped
trying to comb the knots from her hair
nights, when the candles sputter
like some bright notion she's about
to lose. His seed is scattered
in so many nymphs, it's no surprise
that half the babies born
on distant islands look like him,
though they think different thoughts and
cannot bear his name. The son he spawned
in legal loins is out for him, inheritor
of his mother's fond obsession. The others
turn away from him, without a blink
of recognition—black eyes, exactly
his, black as the ripe olives
pressed for oil, that endless flow
that keeps the great wheels wet

and turning, cutting grooves across the back
of earth; everywhere, the burning towns.

Odysseus has returned. And the men
who sailed with him? All lost
or drowned. He's stopped his ears
so he won't hear them calling, men
tossed into the waves like coins
to appease some hypothetical Poseidon.
Their sound keeps breaking
on the shore—the voices of the drowned,
the unrenowned, the living tide
incessant, whispering: anonymous,
anonymous, anonymous . . . the foam
left on the stones when the waves
withdraw—transparent roe, ghost spawn,
it glitters for a moment and is gone.

It is the morning after
Odysseus' return. The suitors lie in heaps
like so much garbage, the flies
already thick. Outside the great gate
of his house in Ithaca, a wailing
like a siren call—the women
with their urns, empty, asking
for the ashes of their sons, their lovers,
something, even a word.
But the shutters of the great house stay closed
against the hot Greek sun. The women
turn at last to go, to glean
the fields, to make strange beds, whatever
kind of home they can invent.
Only Penelope holds her own man
in her arms, the man who left her
to her thoughts all these years.

What she thinks now
is hers alone, Odysseus the intruder.

For those who don't like endings, let the story lift
like ruffled feathers in the wind,
refuse to settle. And let
the not-quite fiction of Penelope
pick up another thread from deep inside her
where the nerves are taut along the bone,
her body like the lute when it is strummed,
from a house that's full
of signals: the slow foot of the cat
upon the stair, the roaches drinking
in the pipes, the hairs that seem to swim
in the washing water, the lizards
rustling in the leaves, the way
that even silence is alive
with premonitions.

Listen. The sound of scissors clicking.
One by one, she cuts the threads
that strung the loom. The shroud
that she'd been weaving
becomes a cloud of falling
shreds, till the room is littered
with useless threads, like sentences
from which the sense had fled.
She shakes her head as if to free it
from the name that she'd repeated
all those years, a litany
for the dead, or an aimless mantra
meant to cover dread—
that frame a gallows
where she had hung, a spider
strangling in its web.

The catch had rusted on the shutters
from disuse. She had to force it.
When she threw the shutters open
it was summer and the sun was high.
As her eyes adjusted to the brilliance
she saw the shape of things outside: a frieze
the wind set into motion, the fields
pouring like an ocean into distance,
the wind-stirred trees, the gate
like someone waiting, the winding road . . .

A knock came at the door and then repeated.
She threw the bolt to buy herself
the time she needed. When he had forced
the door, the room was empty and the loom
stood vacant by the open window.
The sun was blinding: the frame held
only light without an image.

It is not the business of another
to imagine any further. Once she has cut
the long threads of the story, its convenience—
she is free. Abuse *that* word at your peril,
it will return to mock you, like the nameless
who leave their names behind them—
the signatures that spell rebellion,
a freehand scrawl of red graffiti
on the white expensive wall.

THE FOURTH DAVID

for Bob, who gave me the poem

I. Donatello 1430–32: 62¼"

He stands there sleek and calm
and dark in bronze, hardly more
than a boy, his stomach muscles
not yet hard. His poise is slightly
coy; he rests his left foot
on the fallen head as if
it were a hummock in the lawn, overgrown
with matted grass. Relaxed, withdrawn,
his flesh a speaking bronze, denies
base metal, says instead, but softly:
  "please" and promises a pleasure
in its ease. His knees are slightly
bent, his hat is insolent, one soft
hand holds a stone as useless
as a flower; his sword might be
a Hermes wand. Shape-changer,
cool as the poplar's shade
at the crossroads, he stands
above his shield as if he had no need
of it—nude, indolent as May
that ushers in a lassitude
the young have when they only dream
of fame. His name is David;
he wears it lightly as the air
wears dawn. His hair hangs loose,
as careless as men are before
they know how they arouse

the giant, out there,
drowsing naked in the sun.

II. Michelangelo 1501–04: 17′5″

And now he feels the weight
of stone. His body, older, has grown
muscular and tense; he broods
the consequence of playing out
a part he never wanted, he who loves
the lyre and the lamb. He is enormous
in his sex, as if his power
were boulder-born, quarried by a hand
whose veins were throbbing with
a blood they barely could contain,
as if to act were risking floods
of red whose flow would make a river
meager. His pride demands
more than his heart can bear, Hamlet
standing in the hall by a tree stump
like an auger; doubt worms its way
across his brow and furrows it—
a freshly harrowed field
uncertain of its crop. He is a giant
who knows the power he holds in his hand
is only his until
he lets the stone go from the sling.

III. Bernini 1693: life-size

Stand back. The time is past
all hesitation. His eye is fixed: the enemy
is in its center—out there, in the space
he wants to enter; behind him you can hear
the awful anthems and the armies crowding out the light.
His face too set and sharp, too hard
to be a boy's; his sex is draped, his body

shaped now for a different use:
to loose the stone is all, his will
is stone, the figure poised to follow.
The sling is stretched, the rock
is in his hand, his body twisted with
the torsion of the throw.
All his force is focused on tomorrow's
crown; nothing will stop him now.
Intolerable to watch
the slow unfolding of the marble
arms and feel already in your bones
the body of the giant toppling
like a forest through the years
until it's sprawled out on a field
from which the shade's been hacked, the limbs
and trunk from which the leafy head
is missing—discarded weight
that once set matter into motion
and dreamed a ceiling with an infinite recession
of heavy angels toward a filmy light like God.

IV. *Anonymous 1979*

Bronze will not soon speak again
in such sweet tones, nor stone relent
before the sculptor's hand.
How long ago it seems, just past
the flood, the last surviving pair
obeyed the oracle of Themis and restored
the human form by throwing the bones
of earth, the stones, behind them
as they crossed the desolate and flood-torn
plain. And stone grew warm and turned
to flesh, its veins began to pulse
with life, and only something flinty
in the heart retained the memory
of stone, that David loosed—

dead aim, the king who set the stone
in history's sling, and time's
the long slow transit back to granite.

At the museum gate, mute pipes of iron
stand against the sky. Beside them,
on a shaft ten stories tall,
a mobile made of burnished steel
turns in the wind, and turns again
in the dark mirror of the museum wall.
A child, call him David,
plays nearby in the sand. He looks up once
at the towering iron art, these giants
of an alien design, and turns away
and takes his mother's hand
and says, in a voice too small for anyone
but her to understand, "Now
can we go home?"

MY MOTHER'S PORTRAIT

for Gertrude Sherby Rand, 1913–1958

I.

Those sumptuous, lacquered oils, a renaissance
begun too late, too many years waiting
for the children to grow, a husband
to come home to dinner, the sheets waiting
to be folded, those monograms of silk
a shimmer in the cupboard.
There was silver to be shined
and lined up in the china closet,
the socks to be rolled and stored,
dark cashmere fists, in drawers.
So many years of lining shelves, the blue gleam
of washable paper, the polish on exquisite
French provincial, the clock's enamel face
ticking to the wall.

So when the canvases began
to glow with color, it was already so late,
so many centuries since the brush
was trained to follow the eye exactly, the slightest
glimmer of candlelight on a velvet drape,
a touch of ochre to a flushed pink cheek
soon to be varnished over, the elaborate gilt-edged
frames waiting, piled gaping against
the studio walls. So many people wanted to be painted;
unconsciously she flattered them, enhanced
the faces that she saw
with hazel eyes perhaps a shade too loving.

II.

As the years, like brush strokes, built their patina
of early age, objects began to pile up
on the neat white space, became at last
a clutter: under the table, with its carved legs
and sculptured-marble top, cramped space
began to fill, dissembled order, came more and more
to a confusion of brushes held, like a bouquet,
in a cup of India brass. The Renoir lady smiled forever
in her summer wicker chair. The precious little girl
copied from the cover of the Sunday magazine,
defiant in mauve layers of gauze skirt, stood
with her black mary janes catching the broken light
like the skin of lacquered eels. The soft blur
of pastel children's faces . . . the smell of fixative.
Some teacher who had tried to coax a freer form
but failed, had left a canvas of his own, an exercise
in flight, an explosion of birds, the sharp yellow
of beaks in a flurry of white feathers.

But the work stayed real in the old way, each detail
lovingly rendered and attended to, more and more
details, too much to remember, piling up
in a Victorian crescendo—no place
to breathe, the smoky vistas disappeared,
the foreground grew until it blotted out
even the pale *sfumato* of horizon.

III.

Then her studio was empty, the paintings
portioned out to the remaining sisters.
And I don't know what happened to the half-squeezed
tubes of paint, the carefully cleaned brushes,
the little table with the marble top.
I don't know what happened to the years

it took the children to grow up in.
Nor how I could atone for that postponement,
those portraits piled up inside
like courtiers waiting
for an audience with an absent queen.

Sometimes I think for her that I continue—
break up the frames, disband the court, send home
the sycophants who want their likenesses enlarged,
announce, for her, an abdication . . .
and we go off together with our easels
to the open fields
where the birds wheel in the watercolor sky
and the crazy wheat walks blazing into autumn.

IV.

I've only made another picture, tinted
the old print of a dream. Another mother
for the gallery of loss, that wall.
I need an instrument more blunt—
a palette knife to scrape away
these longings, scrape through, be done
with portraiture, soft words like that.
Scrape, scrape away until the light pours through.

And I'd let go those painted Russian dolls
that keep repeating themselves, smaller
each time, these images diminished by
regression, until they're nothing
but an eyeless button.
The snail's path, the winding roads of pearl,
turn back until one day they're finished.
Then the snail has her house and must move,
trailing silver, on. Silent, feeding
on the leaves that give her cover.

Sometimes loss unravels slowly over years,
the old cord, the shed skin of a snake.
Those tribes where the navel cord
is left out in the sun to dry,
the wound to heal in a pucker of rose.
And the snake enters the grass
that has no path, no line can follow.
The brush turns silently to underbrush.
Everything loved is lost and free
to go its way, no tracks,
no turning
back, *yisborach, v'yishtabach, v'yispoar* . . .

LABYRINTH

—sila ersinarsinivdluge

You've lost the clue—somewhere
in the maze, the golden thread's
run out . . . and the air
is getting thick and grainy as old film,
filling with something foul and dank
as steam rising in the heat
from a heap of compost: the animal's lair
is just ahead, the thread's out,
you'll have to go it alone and chance
what's there. The walls have narrowed
to a channel, damp to the hands
that grope your way; the rank air
hangs against the stone, as if
the stone had hooks and held it.
You can't stay where you stand; in the dark
ahead you hear the snorting
and the dull report of hoofs
moved restlessly in place, and then
the corner's rounded. You feel it first
before you see it, and know you've found
the chamber. It is a widening in the stone
lit by a feeble light
that's lost its force from filtering
down the deep rock chimney
from the sky, a sky that's so remote
it's dwindled to this sickly glimmer.
The floor that opens out around you
is spread with straw, in places worn almost
to dust that rises from the ground

where something stamps and stumbles
in its place; the cloud obscures
its shape, postpones
the moment when you'll have to face it.

As a beast will suddenly stiffen at the scent
of someone unexpectedly about, there is
the silence of held breath, a slow settle
of the dust. Just so it appears, as if
a mist had risen and the moon come out.
You both stand frozen for a moment—
two pairs of eyes take hold
and widen, each to take the other in.

The beast is the color of turning cream,
slender with a fawn's grace, fragile
as gentleness grown old, its large eyes
soft with sorrow, its horns
are ivory candelabra, its worn flanks
scarred with roads like countryside
seen from the air. It neither shrinks back
nor approaches, but waits, as snow just fallen
waits for the wind to shape it to the land.
So, slowly you approach, extend your hand and
let the soft nose sniff it, then touch the velvet
muzzle as you touch a rose, wanting to know
its silk but not to bruise it. And then
you know, and turn to go, and hear the light foot-
falls that follow yours and never falter,
only pausing where you pause
as branching way leads on to way. Somewhere near
you hear the sound of dripping water, slow
and even over stone. You feel a nuzzle
at your shoulder, as if to say
this way, go on. So, sometimes led
and sometimes leading, you go until you feel

the air grow fresher, and there's a filament
of light, a slow unravel of gold
like a ray of sun as it passes through the water.
A moment later, the two of you step
blinking into the shining day.

We stood high above the tree line
where the glacier's edge, touched by sun,
becomes a maze of running streams,
a million veins of silver opened into summer.
We stood a long time there amazed
before we felt the bite of hunger and,
together with the sun, began
the long climb down.

IN MEDIAS RES

Here we are in the midst of things—
the same longings
for a body that would last, the same
slow breaking down of what we are
and learn to love and lose:

there are no fathers in the sky,
no mothers in the earth—for who, if he had
fathered men, would twist them till
they're bent with time as olive trees
that, as they grow more picturesque,
begin to bear hard fruit? And who, being
mother to another being, would
give it a taste of life, then, yawning,
take it back again?

And who's the fool who sexed the stars,
fixed tyrants in the sky—anointed
the staring sun as if it were a king,
appointed the cold moon
a virgin queen, dragging the helpless sea
behind her like a train of panting suitors?
And set the stumbling history of a tribe
into celestial stone? So that we have to pray
a comet down to rid ourselves of those
whose madness put them on the throne,
who buy with a legion's death
a night or two of feasting in a rented hall.
Who goes there weeping at the vast
inhuman panoply of stars? Or mourns the passing

of the gods who, if something like ourselves,
are more corrupt than any drought
that merely signifies the absence of the rain.

Today then let us build a temple to the stars
we see above us now, burned out
ten million years ago; hosannas
to the wind that shifts the silent dunes
without intent; and amen to the deep rot
of the forest floor, the subatomic world
we'll never see, the sweet collisions
and the million accidents of time
that gave us life—and all those miracles,
indifferent and inhuman as the waves
that Adam in his garden never dreamed
because they're no more kin
to him than heaven is to kings
or what is natural to what is named.

For what we love we can't call
names—what calls to us
in medias res, that thick green sedge
by the river, and we suppose it
as a bird, though what it is, is
singing.

EX LIBRIS

By the stream, where the ground is soft
and gives, under the slightest pressure—even
the fly would leave its footprint here
and the paw of the shrew the crescent
of its claws like the strokes of a chisel
in clay; where the lightest chill, lighter
than the least rumor of winter, sets the reeds
to a kind of speaking, and a single drop of rain
leaves a crater to catch the first silver
glint of sun when the clouds slide away
from each other like two tired lovers,
and the light returns, pale, though brightened
by the last chapter of late autumn:
copper, rusted oak, gold aspen, and the red
pages of maple, the wind leafing through to the end
the annals of beech, the slim volumes
of birch, the elegant script of the ferns . . .

for the birds, it is all
notations for a coda, for the otter
an invitation to the river,
and for the deer—a dream
in which to disappear, light-footed
on the still open book of earth,
adding the marks of their passage,
adding it all in, waiting only
for the first thick flurry of snowflakes
for cover, soft cover that carries
no title, no name.

FROM
MAYA (1979)

LANDING

It was a pure white cloud that hung there
in the blue, or a jellyfish on a waveless
sea, suspended high above us.
It seemed so effortless in its suspense,
perfectly out of time and out of place
like the ghost of moon in the sky
of a brilliant afternoon.
After a while it seemed to grow, and we
inferred that it was moving, drifting down—
though it seemed weightless, motionless,
one of those things that defy
the usual forces—gravity, and wind
and the almost imperceptible
pressure of the years. But it was coming
down.

      The blur of its outline slowly cleared:
it was scalloped at the lower edge, like a shell
or a child's drawing of a flower, detached
and floating, beauty simplified. That's when
we saw it had a man attached, suspended
from the center of the flower, a kind of human
stamen or a stem. We thought it was
a god, or heavenly seed, sent
to germinate the earth
with a gentler, nobler breed. It might be
someone with sunlit eyes and a mind of dawn.
We thought of falling to our knees.

So you can guess
the way we might have felt

when it landed in our field
with the hard thud of solid flesh
and the terrible flutter of the collapsing
lung of silk. He smelled of old sweat,
his uniform was torn, and he was tangled
in the ropes, hopelessly harnessed
to the white mirage that brought him down.
He had a wound in his chest, a red
flower that took its color from his heart.

We buried him that very day, just as he came
to us, in a uniform of soft brown
with an eagle embroidered on the sleeve,
its body made of careful gray stitches,
its eye a knot of gold. The motto
underneath had almost worn away.
Afterwards, for days, we saw
the huge white shape of silk shifting
in the weeds, like a pale moon
when the wind filled it, stranded,
searching in the aimless way
of unmoored things
for whatever human ballast gave
direction to their endless drift.

UNSTRUNG

Or set upon a golden bough to sing
To lords and ladies of Byzantium
Of what is past, or passing, or to come.

It was a jeweled tapestry:
cut rubies hung for fruit
from the trees; lilies sewn into the ground;
the eyes of the unicorn were pearl
his horn a twist of ivory
his mane a fringe of silk.
The lady was all brocade and lace
her feet impossibly small in scarlet stuff
a satin band around her waist
divided her neatly in two.
The moon was a cluster of seed pearls—
a silver pomegranate with the skin half-gone.
The toy dog's tongue was a shameless red
as if the blood had run into the thread
dyed beyond the possibility of death.
And the eye of the little bird
glittered more impatiently than gems;
it tried its beak on its own gold coat
that tied it to the branch—tore it,
stitch by stitch, to shreds
and danced in its naked bones, fragile
as the structure of a dream or the anatomy
of lace; its call, a drop of rain
sliding down a single silver wire.
It flew into the night—a stroke
or two of chalk wiped off a slate.

The clock strikes; the bony spire of the church
is a black splinter
in the dead white thumb of moon.
The mouse comes out to forage for its young
looks up and sees with widening eyes
the bat, who cannot see
as it sinks its teeth in trembling fur
a face so like its own.

BAILING OUT: A POEM FOR THE SEVENTIES

Whose woods these are I think I know . . .

The landings had gone wrong; white silk
like shrouds, covered the woods.
The trees had trapped the flimsy fabric
in their web—everywhere the harnessed bodies
hung—helpless, treading air
like water.
           We thought to float down
easily—a simple thing,
like coming home: feet first,
a welcome from the waiting fields,
a gentle fall in clover.

We hadn't counted on this
wilderness, the gusts of wind
that took us over; we were surprised
by the tenacity of branching wood,
its reach, and how impenetrable
the place we left, and thought we knew,
could be.
           Sometimes now, as we sway, unwilling
pendulums that mark the time,
we still can dream
someone will come and cut us down.
There is nothing here but words, the calls
we try the dark with—hoping for a human
ear, response, a rescue party.
But all we hear is other

voices like our own, other bodies
tangled in the lines.
the repetition of a cry from every tree:

I can't help you, help me.

EPITAPH

Though only a girl,
the first born of the Pharaoh,
I was the first to die.

Young then,
we were bored already,
rouged pink as oleanders
on the palace grounds, petted
by the eunuchs, overfed
from gemencrusted bowls, barren
with wealth, until the hours of the afternoon
seemed to outlast even
my grandmother's mummy, a perfect
little dried apricot
in a golden skin. We would paint
to pass the time, with delicate
brushes dipped in char
on clay, or on our own blank lids.
So it was that day we found him
wailing in the reeds, he seemed
a miracle to us, plucked
from the lotus by the ibis' beak,
the squalling seed of the sacred
Nile. He was permitted
as a toy; while I pretended play
I honed him like a sword.
For him, I was as polished and as perfect
as a pebble in a stutterer's mouth.
While the slaves' fans beat
incessantly as insect wings,
I taught him how to hate

this painted Pharaoh's tomb
this palace built of brick
and dung, and gilded like a poet's
tongue; these painted eyes.

IPHIGENIA, SETTING THE
RECORD STRAIGHT

The towers waited, shimmering just
beyond the edge of vision.
It was only a question
of wind, of the command of trade routes,
a narrow isthmus between two seas, possession
of the gold that men called Helen.
The oldest of adulteries: trade
and art. We were to wait
for the outcome, to see
if we would be the vassals of a king,
or the slaves of slaves.

They never found my grave, who was supposed
to fill their sails, like the skirts of women,
with her charms. Helen, as the second version goes,
had stayed at home; only the echo
of the rustle of her robes
went with Paris to the high-walled town. I
stayed with her to the end, this aunt of mine,
and friend, whose illness drove her husband out the door,
dull-witted Menelaus. When she died
the swans deserted the palace pool
and the torches flared dark
and fitfully. I did not stay for their return,
like that foolish Electra.

I hid in the shrine of Athena—
hearing her, nights, pace overhead
with an iron step, like the sound

of the bronze age ending. The old blind
singer in the forecourt
must have heard her too, but
unlike me, he had to make his living
from his song. She was often sleepless,
as gods will be, and the nights went slow
under her heel's heavy tread.
When she went to stay the arm of
great Achilles, to save my father
for my mother's knife—
I slipped away.

I have just been living, quiet, in this little village
on goats I keep for cheese and sell for wine, unknown—

the praise of me on every lip, the me
my father made up in his mind
and sacrificed for wind.

EAST OF THE SUN, WEST OF THE MOON

She wore the skins of animals,
laced-up boots, a bright babushka
on her head. Every well was full
of witches, and the bodies of men
cried murder, or sweet love.
Icicles hung from the barns
and when she sought her image
in the pond, the ice was blank.
The geese wore a necklace of
frost, and everything shimmered
in the timid sun. The shadows
of the branches were scribbled
on the snow. When she saw
old women, bent back, humping
down the road, she'd run for cover
in the glittering wood, where little birds
chattered like teeth.

It was in such a season, near
a place with a Russian name, the village
gathered in a circle on the snow,
began the dance, slow at first,
boots pounding the frozen earth,
ermine clouds trimming the air.
They had put her in the center
with the bear, the iron chain around his neck
biting deep in the brown fur.
The dance quickened as the sun
caught the tops of firs, the yellow burning
through the green. Looking up, she seemed to see

from the weedy bottom of a well.
And the world spun
in the sun and in the centrifuge
of clan—it was then
the bear broke loose. He rose
until he blotted out the light—
deep in his throat a sound
like the ice breaking up
in the bay outside St. Petersburg,
the thunder of the spring.

They hunted the bear for days,
but could make nothing of his broken
tracks that bent and doubled back,
and disappeared.
                    The girl was a long time
healing. The slash from one wild claw
had slit her face, hairline to chin.
When it closed, it left a seam
like a rope of red; by fall
it was a slender line, indecipherable,
like the road where it vanishes in wood
and you have to turn around
to get back to the village
before dark.

NATURAL HISTORY

We thought our arms
were like the lowest branches
on the trees, that, reaching out,
prevent the tops from growing, grazing stars.
For years, for centuries, we pruned away
the parts permitting touch. First the twigs,
compassionate with buds, then
the whole branch, scarring
the trunk where the sap oozed out, hardened
into amber. And the tops grew
high as spires, so tall you couldn't
hear the birds in them, and when
wind stirred the leaves, the rustle
was so distant—we thought it
angels. We were armless then
as torsos of ancient marbles dug
from sunken ships and set
on pedestals, eloquent with loss, speaking
of an old perfection—some balance struck
between the chisel and the heart.

But lately, there is a tingling where
our fingers used to be: the bright
excruciating pain of blood
returning to the numb.

We are still trying out our stiff new
limbs, touching things the way
the blind read   the language
made   by puncturing
the page,   letting in
the light.

MAYA

The yogi sits on the burning rock, a drying skin
that has shed its snake. His beggar's bowl
is empty as a skull; the sky *nir-vana*, without the wind.
His eyes are waterless and shed
tears neither for the dead nor those
who drag themselves through doors
to start the daily round again.
He is vacant as the space between two stars.
He lets the lion claws of sun
rake him unopposed. Chameleons, mistaking him
for stone, stretch out on him to take the sun
and lose their color to his own.
And still he sits, transparent soul,
a blister on the earth's brown back.

The woman, says the holy man, can never
escape from *maya*; it grows in her like maggots
in tainted meat, and drives her from his holy ground.

She runs, down the grassy path by which she came;
her passage stirs the grass to dancing. *maya*
maya . . . as she goes down, the growth thickens
the green and tangled forest takes her in.
Her skin is like the fawn's—indelibly marked
with sun and shade: in safety, ornament;
in danger, camouflage. When she sinks down
among the twisted vines and sleeps,
the darkness gathers at the center
of her eyes, the pupil of the moon
under a covering of cloud. *maya, maya* . . .

everything is close to everything, the stars
hang among the woven branches of the trees,
the moon is a lantern overgrown with leaves.
The first light rises from the steaming earth,
a heron lifts his head, his long legs
reeds that awkwardly step
out of their roots and walk, as the sun
opens his great yellow eye and lowers
his gaze, veiled by the lashes of the ferns.
A fish with golden scales leaps
through the shadow of the woman
as she bends to drink.

maya, maya . . . this veil is my skin
that hides me from him
who sees nothing.

THE ROUND FISH

with neither bones nor skin
swims in the green haze of a golden sea
shot through with sun that tangles
in the weeds, like the woven filaments
of tapestry. Playful, he skims the tops of waves
like a skipped stone; plumbs the green depths
not as a stone falls, but
as a swimmer dives for his own delight.
On a still night, when you think you see the moon
stare back at you from the surface of a pond,
it may not be a mere reflected light,
twice-removed from the sun—but the round fish
regarding you, as a man may stare intently
at a mirror, trying, through the too familiar face,
to catch a glimpse of someone half-perceived.
It is no trick of mirrors, no infinite regress
of self-regarding mind, but the round fish
regarding you, recovering his own.

I watched a man one night, by a stream,
transfixed by the round fish, until he broke
the water with his hand, wanting to scoop
it out, like some demented bear, all his cunning
in his paw. When he drew back his arm,
his hand was silver to the wrist.

That night I dreamed of swimming, far out
at sea, beyond the line of reefs, easy
as you swim in dreams. And the round fish
with neither bones nor skin

swam near, the sky blazed blue, the fish
was rainbow-hued, right before he disappeared.
Surprised, I saw a jut of land I hadn't seen before
and climbed ashore, following the tracks
the fish had left, which fit so strangely
with my own. The trail now is not so fresh,
harder to follow in the undergrowth; still
it was something to have been started on at all;
it hardly matters that, where the sea turns
into land and the growth thickens—you no longer know
the trail you take
from the one that you are making as you go.

NOTES

New Poems (2011–2017)

"Turning": The lines "but just what, invisible, / calls forth mass / from the passing particles, / and spins a world … " refer to the Higgs boson, popularly referred to as "the God particle." It was once theorized and has lately been shown that there is such a particle and that the Higgs field permeates the whole universe. It is this field that produces mass in the universe; that is, in certain places the field becomes excited, and these excitations show themselves as Higgs particles, which are essential to some conversion process that creates what we think of as mass.

"Homage" is written for Vievee Francis, and in response to her poem "Like Jesus to the Crows" and in appreciation of the book in which it appears, *Forest Primeval* (Northwestern University Press, 2016).

"Wingspan" is for Tony Hoagland, with love. It was written in a *renshi* (poem chain in which the last line of the preceding poem becomes your title) with Rose Auslander and Kim Hamilton; the connection of Hope with "the scope of her short wings" is from the close of Kim's poem, "Tourist Map": "*Charity* with her tray of sugared buns and *Hope* / with her sturdy body swept from stucco and streams / pointing beyond the scope of her short wings."

"Another Allegory of the Cave" is written as an homage to the art of William Kentridge, and in response to his "Drawing Lesson One: In Praise of Shadows," from *Six Drawing Lessons, The Charles Eliot Norton Lectures of 2012* (Harvard University Press, 2014).

"Endings, from a Verse by Gwendolyn Brooks" owes its form to the invention by Terrance Hayes of what became known as the Golden Shovel form, because of the way he employed Ms. Brooks well-known poem, "We Real Cool," whose speakers she identifies as "The Pool Players. / Seven at the

Golden Shovel." Her poem became his poem's right-hand spine, each of her words the last word of each of his lines. The releasing power of this form can be seen in poems by hundreds of poets who contributed to *The Golden Shovel Anthology: New Poems Honoring Gwendolyn Brooks*, edited by Peter Kahn, Ravi Shankar, and Patricia Smith (University of Arkansas Press, 2017).

"Gnawed Bone, Covered Bridge"—The image of the girl gnawing a bone that opens my poem is owed to Jynne Dilling Martin from a poem in her book *We Mammals in Hospitable Times* (Carnegie Mellon, 2015). The image that closes my poem is owed to an image that ends Ross Leckie's poem "Hartland," from *Gravity's Plumb Line* (Gaspereau Press, 2005).

Like "Wingspan," a number of these poems were written in the *renshi* with Rose Auslander and Kim Hamilton. As noted in 3 (above), the *renshi*'s only requirement is that your poem use the last line of another's poem as your title. Sometimes, as the poems evolved, I confess to dropping the original title.

"For the First Time" refers to the Vermont custom, learned from Vermonter and poet Ellen McCulloch-Lovell, of a wandering group whose handbell ringing announces the spring.

"The Uses of What Is Hollow" takes its inspiration from the Greek myth of Pan and Syrinx. The story goes that Pan, the goat-footed, randy nature god, pursued the chaste nymph Syrinx, who, desperate to escape him, called on the river nymphs, who transformed her into a stand of reeds. It was from those reeds that Pan bound together the musical instrument we call the panpipe (or syrinx), one of the earliest woodwind instruments, long associated with the music of shepherds. The poem is especially in memory of Dr. Roger Cole, beloved cousin.

"Ars Poetica, 2017": The poem's opening lines refer to the German poet and dramatist Friedrich Schiller (1759–1805) in the film *Die geliebten Schwestern* ("The Beloved Sisters"), depicting his purported *ménage à trois* with two sisters, and his other love affair—with the French Revolution, referred to later in the poem as "the tri-color dream." As to the amber castle, I was told that Lithuanian mothers give their daughters a gift of amber when they come of age, so that, together, the women reconstitute the amber castle of the Sun Goddess that once stood in the depths of the

Baltic Sea, and that the men destroyed. The girl picking flowers is, of course, Kore, who, abducted by Hades, becomes Persephone, Queen of the Dead, in the Greek seasonal rebirth myth of Demeter and Persephone. Tiresias is from Sophocles' drama *Oedipus Rex*—the blind seer whose wisdom is, as he knows, useless to prevent the tragedy.

from *Tourist in Hell* (2010)

"Magnificat": the title is an ironic reference to the Magnificat or Canticle of Mary, Mary's praise to the power of God in the son she carries, from Luke 1:46–55, sung or recited as part of Christian liturgy.

"Voices from the Labyrinth": These poems had their origin in a request by book artist Enid Mark, with whom I had collaborated before, to write poems for a book on the theme of the Greek myth of the Labyrinth. She did not know, as we set out on this project, that she would herself soon be entering the labyrinth of hospitals and treatments, and would not live to complete the book for which these poems were written, and whose odd shapes were inspired by both their content and her design.

    I hope that the old story is still known: of the Minotaur, half-man and half-bull, lovechild of the Minoan Queen Pasiphae and a bull, hidden away by King Minos in a labyrinth in the palace at Knossos, a maze cunningly devised by Daedalus; of the Greek Theseus, who was sent as tribute from Athens to the powerful Minoan kingdom, and was meant for sacrifice to the ravenous Minotaur; of Minos's daughter Ariadne, who fell in love with Theseus, and gave him a clew (thread) that led him out of the labyrinth after he had killed the Minotaur. But that is only the way Greek myth tells the story. We live a long way from there.

from *The Girl with Bees in Her Hair* (2004)

"Everything Is Starting" is for Marcia Pelletiere.

"What Narcissus Gave the Lake": Its epigraph closes Constance Merritt's poem "Ars Poetica," from *A Protocol for Touch* (University of North Texas Press, 2000).

"Don't look so scared. You're alive!": This title is the last line of a poem in a *renshi* by Amy McNamara. The quoted line, "The dim boy claps because the others clap," is the recurring line in a villanelle, "The Freaks at Spurgin Road Field" by Richard Hugo, from *What Thou Lovest Well, Remains American* (W.W. Norton, 1975.)

"This Straw and Manure World": The title is the last line of a poem by Kathleen Jesme, and is from a *renshi* with Kath and Carlen Arnett.

"Just So Story": The reference to Old Glory "in its fixed imitation of a flag in wind" is literally true. The flag the astronauts planted was constructed with a permanent wave, since the lack of air on the moon meant that a real flag would just ingloriously go limp.

"The Girl with Bees in Her Hair" is for Janet Shaw, who sent the envelope, and is dedicated to the memory of Susan Sontag and all those, like her, reviled for telling the truth.

from *Reversing the Spell, New Poems* (1993–1996)

"*Trümmerfrauen* (The Rubble-Women)": This poem came from the description given by my friend Ingo Regier of his memories as a young boy in Germany at the end of World War II, of passing these women on his way to school as they removed the old mortar from the rubble of the bombed city, preparing the stones to rebuild Germany.

"Facing into It": This poem for Larry Levis was never intended as an elegy. It was written several years before Larry's untimely death.

"The Messenger" was inspired by a man named Pascal. It was transformed into a dance work by Melanie Stewart Dance, music composed by Mick Rossi, and performed at the Arts Bank, Philadelphia, 1996.

"Up Against It": The poem refers to one of the initiating events of the Spanish Civil War, the 1936 murder of the poet Federico García Lorca by Franco's fascist *falangistas* whose battle cry was "*¡Vive La Muerte!*" ("Long Live Death!"). There are several references to translated quotations from García Lorca: when asked what it was to be a poet, Lorca replied: "*yo tengo un fuego en mis manos*" ("I have a fire in my hands"); a well-known poem of his begins with the line "*Si muero, dejad el balcón abierto.*" ("If I die, leave the balcony open.")

from *Otherwise* (1993)

"Night Fishing in the Sound": The closing image "cauldron of dawn" unintentionally but significantly both echoes and reverses the end of Sylvia Plath's poem "Ariel."

"Being As I Was, How Could I Help ... ": The inspiration for this poem was the 1991 dance "Cry Wolf," in which a she-wolf was danced and choreographed by Hellmut Gottschild for his company, Zero Moving.

"The Muse": Jacques Lacan was a French psychoanalyst and literary theorist who identified symbol-making with a certain part of the male anatomy.

"*Ume*: Plum": The pronunciation of *ume* sounds the final e. *Sakura* means both cherry tree and cherry blossom. The emperor of the poem is the late Showa emperor; in his eighties at the time of the poem's action, he had reigned throughout World War II and its aftermath.

"Rhapsody, with Rain": This poem is in memory of poet Sarah Lantz.

from *Sarah's Choice* (1989)

"The Last Man" is dedicated to Vivian Schatz, lifelong activist for peace. And see first note for *Shekhinah*.

"Conversation with a Japanese Student": The word *akarui* means "bright," "luminous." Often used to refer to blue skies, a fine day, its extended meaning denotes the bright time of peace and prosperity in Japan since the 1960s. The quotation in that poem ("A beautiful and charming Female Floating Westward through the air, bearing on her forehead the Star of Empire") appeared in the text on the reverse side of *American Progress*, a popular allegorical print of 1873, referring to the white diaphanous figure presiding over the tides of men, cities, trains, churches, and fleeing before those conquering tides—Native Americans, buffalo and bear, calling it, without irony, "the grand drama of Progress in the civilization, settlement and history of our own happy land."

"High Noon at Los Alamos": The reference in "sentries set to watch / at Argos for the signal fire" is from the opening scene of *Agamemnon* from the *Oresteia* by Aeschylus; it refers to antiquity's long-distance communication—fires lit along a chain of mountains. The sentry in the tragedy was watching for the fire that meant a Greek victory in the Trojan War—the city of Troy defeated and set ablaze.

from *Shekhinah* (1984)

Shekhinah: In Jewish theology, the *Shekhinah* was the merciful, in-dwelling, immanent and feminine aspect of the divine, a figure expunged from the canonical Bible. In various noncanonical sources, the *Shekhinah* was believed to be a mercy cloud that once covered the ark of the covenant but, with the destruction of the Temple, moved with the people of the diaspora. Herman Melville came across it in his study of comparative religion, embraced it as the missing aspect of the wrathful Puritan God, and let it inform *Moby Dick* in important ways. And this informs the end of my poem "The Last Man."

"Emigration": I confess to poetic license in the poem in regard to Charlotte's friend Mary Taylor; she in fact emigrated to New Zealand, but Australia makes a nice slant rhyme with Taylor, and the point, if not the place, is the same.

"Labyrinth": the epigraph *sila ersinarsinivdluge* comes from Joseph Campbell's *The Masks of God*; in this citation Campbell is quoting the shaman Najagneq:

> *Silam* or *Silam inua*, "the inhabitant or soul of the universe," is never seen; its voice alone is heard. "All we know is that it has a gentle voice like a woman, a voice so fine and gentle that even children cannot become afraid. What it says is: *sila ersinarsinivdluge*, 'be not afraid of the universe.'"

from *maya* (1979)

"Unstrung": The often quoted epigraph comprises the last three lines of "Sailing to Byzantium" by William Butler Yeats.